The Thinkers 5(

THE THINKERS
50

*The world's 50
most important and influential
management thinkers*

Ciaran Parker

Foreword by Stuart Crainer and Des Dearlove

London
Business
Press

First published in 2006

London Business Press
Editorial Offices
23 Ruscombe Road
Twyford
Berkshire RG10 9JL
UK

00 44 (0)1342-825328
www.londonbusinesspress.com

ISBN 0-9550085-1-4

Text design and typesetting by Sparks – www.sparks.co.uk
Cover design by Jebens Design – www.jebensdesign.co.uk

Printed and bound in India by Replika Press Pvt. Ltd.

Thank you to Leif Edvinsson, W. Chan Kim and Renée Mauborgne, Vijay Govindarajan, Rob Goffee and Gareth Jones, C.K. Prahalad, Kjell Nordström and Jonas Ridderstråle, Kenichi Ohmae, and Lynda Gratton for permission to reprint photographs. The photograph of Govindarajan is by Gilbert Fox, Nordström and Ridderstråle by Thomas Engstrom, Jones and Goffee by Kim Grace, and Kim and Mauborgne by John Abbott.

CONTENTS

....

FOREWORD

By Stuart Crainer and Des Dearlove

Who is the most influential living management thinker? That was the simple question that inspired the original *Thinkers 50* in 2001. A lot of hard work and number crunching later, the answer became the first global ranking of business gurus. At the time, we had no idea that it would prove so popular – or so influential.

The ranking has now become a bi-annual event. Produced by Suntop Media in association with the European Foundation for Management Development (EFMD), it has become the definitive guide to which thinkers and ideas are in – and which have been consigned to business history. The 2005 ranking forms the basis for the selection in Ciaran Parker's book. Thanks to Parminder Bahra and Carol Lewis, this ranking was published by *The (London) Times* and reached its widest audience yet.

So what does the continued interest in the ranking tell us? For one thing, it tells us that businesspeople care about ideas and the thinkers who generate them. It also tells us that although the world of business – and business ideas – is ever changing, some things remain reassuringly stable. Seven of the top ten thinkers from the original ranking in 2001 are still there – although their positions have altered. The great thinkers are not quickly discarded.

These thinkers and many others have contributed and continue to contribute to a steady flow of new ideas that redefine what managers should be doing, how they should be doing it and, crucially, what their performance is evaluated against. Today's theory is tomorrow's task.

The problem is that in recent years the flow of ideas has become a torrent. This book aims to make life easier by exploring the ideas and thinkers who are significant among the thousands that have emerged. Some of them are new, while others have been around in one form or another for years. We make no apologies for that. Good ideas last long after the fads have evaporated into the hot air from whence they came.

Indeed, a growing problem is the sheer volume of new ideas touted each year as "breakthroughs," new "blueprints for success," or some other over-blown claim. Idea after idea is launched with ever-louder fanfare. And the trumpeting gets more strident. Cynicism is reaching epidemic proportions.

Many of the buzzwords ring hollow. If anything, the credibility gap is widening. People feel disconnected from the language of management. It can seem surreal. The irreverent observations of Dilbert and Dogbert have already made their creator Scott Adams the best-selling business author in the world – and made him a fixture in the Thinkers 50 (www.thinkers50. com). The excessive use of buzzwords undermines serious business ideas. The people who use them are often fashion victims.

"It's part of the fad cycle," notes MIT's Peter Senge, whose place in the top 50 remains secure, and whose book *The Fifth Discipline* popularized the phrase "learning organization." "People consume then drop fads and ideas all the time and corporations are no different."

Such is the cynicism that now exists among some parts of the business press that there is little real attempt to decipher those with something impor-tant to say from the merely mellifluous. There is little in the way of quality control. As a result, managers have been deluged with ideas. In a business world where information overload is already a major cause of stress, the choice is either a desperate attempt to read and assimilate everything – or ignore it altogether.

Most managers are caught in the middle, reading what they can when they can and trying to sort the nuggets from the rest. We hope the Thinkers 50 can help them in that task.

This is a book for anyone and everyone who cares about business and the ideas that are shaping it today, tomorrow, and into the future.

Des Dearlove and Stuart Crainer, London, January 2006
www.thinkers50.com

RUSSELL ACKOFF

Educator (2005 Ranking: 26)

Russell L. Ackoff was born in Philadelphia in 1919. He studied architecture at the University of Pennsylvania but, after graduation, his interest turned to the philosophy of science, in which he gained a doctorate. He explains that he was "more interested in people-oriented systems than in buildings" and this led to an interest in operations research.

He held a professorship at the Case Institute of Technology in Cleveland, Ohio, until he returned to his alma mater, the University of Pennsylvania, in 1964. Although he is now retired from formal teaching, he still holds the Anheuser Busch Emeritus Professorship in Management Science at the Wharton School of Business. He has also consulted widely; he is the founder and chairman of the Philadelphia-based INTERACT: The Institute for Interactive Management Inc.

Russ Ackoff's interests have always been extensive. They range from human behavior to town planning. He has always been interested in systems, devising ways of describing how (and often why) organizations work or do not work. This led to his co-authoring *Introduction to Operations Research* (1957). Although the concept of operations or operational research had been the subject of inquiry since World War II, this was the first work to point to the contributions the discipline could make to the world of business, specifically industrial manufacturing. All systems, even the most complex and apparently chaotic, were based on the organization and manipulation of inputs, preferably towards the production of desirable outputs. The more complex the system, the greater the number of inputs and possible variables that emerge.

As well as leading to a string of further publications, Ackoff's operations research spawned the creation of a new channel of debate among business thinkers. Ackoff has often been described as the dean of systems thinking. His alma mater's School of Engineering even established a think tank named the Center for the Advancement of Systems Approaches (A-CASA) named in his honor. The availability of cheaper and yet more powerful computers led to a related breakthrough: because of a computer's ability to plot and track systems, even the most modest organization could benefit from the blessings of operations research. Ackoff always felt that operations research was more than the mere quantification of activity. It was, he believed, a way to better gauge how an organization (and the people in it) really worked.

His writing and lecturing have frequently been marked by caustic wit. Ackoff felt that operations research had not been fully deployed, that it was used with only partial understanding and, thus, minimal results. Alternatively, as Ackoff might have phrased it, operations research had led to corporate constipation. Instead of being allowed to reside in the organizational cranium, it had been progressively pushed down into the organizational bowels. Extending the analogy, he stated that when it could no longer be pushed down it was pushed out. Ackoff was never one for political correctness when it came to management issues.

In fact, Ackoff has always liked challenging convention. At Wharton, his program had "no curriculum, no classes, no examinations, no admission requirements – only exit requirements – in which the students designed their own education, not only the content but the process of it." His approach had its critics to whom he responded: "[T]he worst thing you can do for the long run is to be successful while breaking rules. You can fail as much as you want to, as long as you follow the rules." In terms of managing a business, he worries that the Internet has led to an overabundance of misinformation, or at the very least, irrelevant information.

Recently, he has turned his attention to other areas of society, such as education. He has called for the elimination of teacher education colleges because he believes teaching often obstructs student learning.

In *Re-Creating the Corporation* (1999) he comments on the decline in the corporate age limit. He argues that corporations must forget functional divisions and get all sections singing from the same hymnal. They must plan and design effectively, and they must introduce authentic internal democracy.

They must learn on the hoof and adapt as they learn, never forgetting that the future belongs to the flexible. In *Redesigning Society* (2003) Ackoff attempts to provide solutions to America's problems through using operations research. He asserts, "It is only through creative thought and innovation that our society will be transformed ..."

Other recent publications include *Beating the System: Using Creativity to Outsmart Bureaucracies* (2005), a witty collection of anecdotes that sets out to confront abusive and officious behavior. Some of his most enduring and idiosyncratic writings are contained in *Ackoff's Best* (1998).

Essential reading

http://www.acasa.upenn.edu/advisory.htm

Introduction to Operations Research (Wiley, 1957) (with C. W. Churchman and E. L. Arnoff)

Ackoff's Best: His Classic Writings on Management (Wiley, 1998)

Re-Creating the Corporation: A Design of Organizations for the 21st Century (Oxford University Press, 1999)

Redesigning Society (Stanford University Press, 2003) (with Sheldon Rovin)

Beating the System: Using Creativity to Outsmart Bureaucracies (Berrett-Koehler, 2005)

SCOTT ADAMS
Author and Cartoonist (2005 Ranking: 12)

Scott Adams (born 1957) is the inventor of Dilbert, a character who has debunked a lot of the fog about the workplace. In plain language, work is still a four-letter word.

Adams was born in the Catskill Mountains in New York State. He got an economics degree from Hartwick College and an M.B.A. from UCLA Berkeley. He worked at Crocker National Bank and then Pacific Bell. He started more or less at the bottom, as a bank teller (where he was held up twice at gunpoint), but began a gradual ascent up the corporate pyramid. This was a journey he found underwhelming, especially the long and inconclusive meetings. He was frequently bored out of his tree. Instead of turning to counseling, drugs or booze he made creative use of this mental down-time, drawing satirical and grotesque caricatures and cartoons of those around him. One four-eyed character started to stand out from the crowd in his material. He christened him "Dilbert."

In 1988 he submitted some of the *Dilbert* sketches to the big cartoon syndicates. They were snapped up by United Feature Syndicate. In 1989 *Dilbert* was syndicated in 50 newspapers. Today the figure is more than 1,500. Dilbert was soon available in a book format. With the rise of the Internet, *Dilbert* went cyber. Adams kept his day job with Pacific Bell until 1995. He has since devoted himself to drawing, giving talks, and writing. One of the products has been *The Dilbert Principle* (1996). This stated what most people knew and felt but had probably been too afraid to say.

Satire as a literary form has a long history. No form of human activity can ever escape it for long, so modern management and its absurdities was bound to find its satirist. Each age throws up its own clash of incongruities between individual and collective, the stated ideal and the observed reality, not to mention the tension between a world that everyone says is becoming like heaven on earth but is usually becoming more like hell on earth. There is the clash between the introvert and the extrovert, the retiring type and the person whose ego could fill a football stadium. There is always a need to debunk, for the little boy courageous enough to say, "The Emperor's wearing no clothes." This is what *The Dilbert Principle* is about.

Dilbert is not overtly political. It is not saying that things should be done in a particular way. It does not say that the corporate world where many people work is inherently evil. It's just stupid a lot of the time. *The Dilbert Principle* is about laughing and poking, and, at the end of the day, coping. People in organizations are faced with two different yet linked realities. They are both crucial. People flit from one to the other to survive.

Adams followed up with *Dogbert's Management Handbook* (1997). Here the voice of the management guru is transferred from Dilbert to his canine best friend Dogbert.

Many management gurus preach the need to make the workplace fun. Humor reduces stress and aids productivity. Some companies employ humor consultants. However, it can never be enforced. Laughter is still distrusted by many. It is ambiguous. It is all right while everyone is laughing together, but what if subordinates are laughing *at* management instead of with them?

Recent output from Adams includes stuff that is not Dilbert-related, and for many, not even funny. Examples include the "thought experiment," *God's Debris* (2004).

Scott Adams is still a licensed hypnotist.

Essential reading

http://www.dilbert.com
The Dilbert Principle: A Cubicle's-Eye View of Bosses, Meetings, Management Fads & Other Workplace Afflictions (Collins, 1996)
Dogbert's Management Handbook (Collins, 1997)
It's Not Funny If I Have to Explain It: A Dilbert Treasury (Andrews McMeel, 2004)

CHRIS ARGYRIS
Educator (2005 Ranking: 28)

....

Chris Argyris was born in Newark, New Jersey, in 1923. After service in World War II he studied psychology at Clark University. He pursued post-graduate studies in psychology and economics at Kansas University, eventually earning a Ph.D. in Organizational Behavior at Cornell. He was Beach Professor of Organizational Sciences at Yale before moving to the faculty at Harvard, where he is currently James Bryan Conant Professor of Education and Organizational Behavior. He is the author of nearly 20 books and many articles. He is a director of Monitor consulting company.

Argyris was the first to write about "the learning organization." It was his pupil, Peter Senge, who brought the term to a much wider audience through his book *The Fifth Discipline* (1990).

Argyris' early research concentrated on organizational control systems and how individuals responded to these. This resulted in *Personality and Organization* (1957). He later studied the impact of change on an organization, especially on top-level management, in books like *Organizations and Innovation* (1970).

In the 1970s he developed, along with the late Donald Schön, a new theory of motivation based on unique "mind maps." They called them "theories-in-use"; these inform individuals about how to respond to situations. They are not always visible, because many people feel compelled to defend their behavior by reference to a more acceptable "mind map." Argyris termed this "espoused thought." Personal effectiveness depended on lessening the gap between these two mind maps.

For Argyris, learning proceeds from making mistakes and correcting them. He identified frameworks or governing variables that determined how people corrected errors. In an environment in which things like values are strong and strategies are taken for granted, answers to mistakes are sought within the existing framework. Argyris calls this "single-loop" learning. It tends to be self-sustaining and psychologically comforting. If, on the other hand, the governing variables are rejected and novel answers to problems are sought instead, "double-loop learning" occurs. This is more valuable for the organization in times of change.

Argyris then described the implications this had for organizations. "Single-loop" learning often inhibits creativity and "double-loop" thinking. Both originated in different mind maps. Argyris called them Model I (single loop) and Model II (double loop). His research has found that Model I theories predominate. These are further characterized by:

+ Defensiveness
+ Hiding and denying uncomfortable information
+ Avoiding negativity
+ A need to win at all costs
+ Worshipping rational behavior and decrying anything that doesn't conform or seems left field
+ "Of course I'm right" attitudes

In Model II mind maps there is emphasis on:

+ Dialogue
+ Sharing tasks and information
+ Free choice based on valid information
+ Questioning of assumptions

There is a need to move people from Model I to Model II selection. Neither takes prisoners, nor can co-exist in an organization.

No matter which mind map holds sway, the people in the organization need to know all about it and their part within it. The dominant mind map is reflected in the organization as a whole. One in which Model I calls the shots is defensive. It relies on self-fulfilling prophecies and is learning-challenged.

Errors and problems are never properly fixed. The solution? An organization dominated by Model II, double-loop thinking. Members learn by reflecting critically. Easy? Well, not really. Model II organizations are still rare; their scarcity is bemoaned by Argyris.

Argyris has been frustrated at how little impact his theories have had on management. He knows managers pay lip service to pursuing double-loop thinking. In reality they prefer the comfort zone of single looping. He puts much of this down to training and self-delusion. There are companies that know their problems and their weakness in learning, but they choose to ignore them. It is only those companies that know how best to use their employees' talents more effectively that can hope to prosper.

Essential reading

http://www.actionscience.com/index.htm

Theory in Practice: Increasing Professional Effectiveness (Jossey-Bass, 1974) (with Donald Schön)

Organizational Learning (Addison Wesley, 1978) (with Donald Schön)

Overcoming Organizational Defenses (Prentice Hall, 1990)

Flawed Advice and the Management Trap: How Managers Can Know When They're Getting Good Advice and When They're Not (Oxford University Press, 1999)

Reasons and Rationalizations: The Limits to Organizational Knowledge (Oxford University Press, 2004)

WARREN BENNIS

Educator (2005 Ranking: 27)

Warren G. Bennis (born 1925) is currently University Professor and Distinguished Professor of Business Administration at the Marshall School of the University of Southern California (USC), and is founding chairman of USC's Leadership Institute.

Bennis saw military action in Europe in the closing phases of World War II. At the age of 20 he became one of the youngest infantry commanders in the U.S. Army and was decorated with the Purple Heart. This is where he probably became interested in leadership, an interest that has remained with him throughout his life.

He worked as an adviser to four U.S. presidents, ranging from John F. Kennedy to Ronald Reagan. According to Bennis, leadership is all about unlocking individual talents and combining them for the good of all.

He taught on the faculties of Harvard and the University of Boston. He also worked at MIT's Sloan School of Management as chairman of the Organizational Studies Department. Sensing a need to experience the joys and frustrations of leadership first hand, he left to take up a post in college administration, first as vice president of the State University of New York at Buffalo, and then as president of the University of Cincinnati.

Bennis has written over 25 books, nearly all with a common theme (often mentioned in the title) – leadership. The two most successful volumes to date have been *Leaders* (1986) and *On Becoming a Leader* (1989). Both have been translated into 20 languages.

Leaders resulted from interviews with 90 leaders, two-thirds of them from the corporate world. It was not meant to be a work of scientific analysis, brimming with charts and statistics. Bennis never pontificates on leadership. The leaders he interviewed were in their own way very different people with their own styles of leadership.

He believes that the business leader should have a number of necessary skills. These are:

+ Vision: an idea of where he or she is going – and leading others
+ Passion: the means of spreading belief among others
+ Integrity: those who are led must be able to invest trust (or money) in the leader's vision
+ Curiosity: an unwillingness to be satisfied with the mundane and the everyday
+ Courage: a sense of daring and a willingness to take risks

A leader also has to be able to cope with criticism, using it when valid.

In the 1990s Bennis broadened his analysis of leadership. Part of this was due to the changed circumstances of the business world. Leadership was easier when there was a nice tidy group of loyal followers. When dealing with a flatter and more amorphous collective, it gets much harder. Leaders should still lead from the front, but in the messed-up world of today it is hard to find where the front is, let alone the back or the middle. He looked at how the nature of leadership was changing in an era or environment of uncertainty. He speaks as much about partnership as about leadership. He has also looked at the strengths that leadership can gain from good cooperation in *Organizing Genius* (1997), *Co-Leaders* (1999), and *Managing the Dream* (2000). In the first of these he examined some examples of teamwork from history, such as the Manhattan Project and the developers of the Apple Macintosh computer. Although each group is unique, they have certain coincidences. There is a determination to work for common goals and, often, to make huge personal sacrifices. However, even in these collectives there is still a need for a leading figure. He or she reminds the others to keep their eyes on the prize. This type of leader helps them keep on going when they hit rough patches or snags, or even acts as a type of protector from the outside world.

The theater-loving Bennis is a very widely read man. This shows up in the multitude of quotations throughout his work. His biography on the USC Marshall faculty Web page mentions a still unsatisfied ambition to write a "really good one-act play." He is fond of the pithy aphorism: "The manager is a copy: the leader is an original" or the equally memorable "The good manager does things right. The good leader does the right thing." These have entered the liturgy of management theory. This is more than verbal grandstanding. It encapsulates an essential message in a few words. For Bennis, management and leadership are different tasks.

Essential reading

http://www.usc.edu/programs/cet/faculty_fellows/bennis.html
Leaders (Harper & Row, 1986) (with Bert Nanus)
On Becoming a Leader (Perseus, 1989)
Organizing Genius: The Secrets of Creative Collaboration (Perseus, 1997) (with Patricia Ward Biederman)

JEFF BEZOS

Founder and CEO of Amazon.com

(2005 Ranking: 40)

Jeff Bezos was born in Albuquerque, New Mexico in 1963. As a boy Jeff was good with numbers and gadgets. He tried – unsuccessfully – to make a hovercraft out of a vacuum cleaner. He studied computer science and electronic engineering at Princeton. After graduation, he worked in New York, soon becoming senior vice president at the investment firm D. E. Shaw at the tender age of 28.

According to Bezos, one day in the mid-1990s he stumbled over the fact that the Web was growing by an amazing 2,300 percent per month! It was big and growing bigger – it had huge potential, but for what?

Bezos was well placed to take the Internet on to the next level. He was the rare combination of a Wall Street insider and a techno super-literate. He was not the first to realize the Web could be used for a type of high-tech mail order. He drew up a short list of potential products. Books were interesting. Unlike the music industry, dominated by six companies, the American publishing and book retailing market was fairly open. There were big names there, but none of them had a stranglehold on market share. "There were no 800-pound gorillas in book publishing or distribution." There were also far more units: 1.3 million books versus 300,000 music titles. High velocity would be a key to success. There were also warehouses big enough to store all the books available.

Bezos decided to go for it. He gave up his job with all its certainties for the uncertainty of a new business adventure. He had to relocate. New ideas need space, and New York was just too crowded. Even he did not know exactly where he was going, but he promised to phone once he got there. He set off westwards with his wife Mackenzie and their golden retriever in their Chevrolet Blazer.

On the surface this move had something of the epic about it, like Moses going into the Promised Land. It also seemed similar to the American pioneers in their covered wagons moving west in previous centuries, battling hostile Indians and the vicissitudes of nature. Bezos might have been a visionary, but he was no gambler with fortune. There were no hostile Indians, and the weather service advised travelers of inclement weather. He didn't need a carbine, but he did have a laptop computer and a cellular phone. He was able to contact potential investors and formulate business plans on the journey.

His idea was novel: *a huge bookstore in cyberspace*. Investors were cautiously unimpressed. "If I had a nickel for every time a potential investor told me this wouldn't work …" His idea had certain attractions, though. There wouldn't be a need for conventional bricks-and-mortar bookstores. Staff costs would be lower. The savings could be passed on to the consumer in lower prices. Eventually enough investors bought into his idea.

His base would be Washington State in the U.S. northwest, already a high-tech magnet. The company started modestly enough: three employees in a garage. It adopted the name "Amazon" because of the links with a huge ever-changing river.

Within a few years of its establishment Amazon had transformed book buying. Not only did it offer cheaper prices, but it also offered them to buyers in the comfort of their own home. It soon realized the value of customer participation, encouraging book reviews and wish lists. Amazon was able to change the buying experience. Amazon never forgot purchasers' habits. The more you visited the site, the more it knew (or thought it knew) about your buying habits and preferences.

Amazon has subsequently diversified into music, DVDs and consumer electronics, cars, holiday gifts, and toys. Bezos has signaled his ambition for Amazon to become the ultimate retail outlet, selling anything to anybody.

Amazon went public in 1997. The relationship between Amazon and its stock price has often been paradoxical. The former lost money for years, but that did not seem to have an impact on the latter. The shares dipped by a fifth in Q4 of 2001 – when Amazon made its first profits. This encapsulates how e-commerce had changed the world. If you've got a great idea, it doesn't seem to matter if you lose money at first.

Jeff Bezos is a man of faith in the future. He does not take himself too seriously. Maybe that is why he has yet to put his ideas and experience in management into book form. Maybe he hasn't had time.

Essential reading

http://phx.corporate-ir.net/phoenix.zhtml?c=97664&p=irol-govBio &ID=69376

LARRY BOSSIDY

Executive (2005 Ranking: 48)

Lawrence A. Bossidy was born in Pittsfield, Massachusetts, in 1934. After working in a local shoe store during his youth, he studied economics at Colgate University in New York State. In 1957 he joined General Electric (GE) as a trainee. He rose steadily through the ranks, occupying numerous executive positions. He became successively: chief operating officer of General Electric Credit Corporation (now GE Capital Corporation), executive vice president and president of GE's Services and Materials Sector, and finally vice chairman and executive officer of General Electric. In 1991 he became chairman and CEO of Allied Signal.

True to his GE heritage, he was motivated by the ideas of Six Sigma strategy. This emphasis on growth was reflected in healthy financial returns. In 1999 Allied Signal merged with Honeywell, and Bossidy stayed on as chairman. One year later he retired – but came back a few months later as chairman and CEO of Honeywell International. This came in the wake of a failed takeover bid from his former employer, GE. He was invited to return to the Honeywell helm for a year so as to "get the company back on track." He retired for a second time in 2002. Today, he is a well-known speaker and lecturer and serves on numerous boards, including the Business Roundtable. His most noteworthy achievement since retirement has probably been his co-authorship of two best-selling management strategy books with his colleague, fellow management thinker, and corporate coach, Ram Charan.

The first of these, *Execution: The Art of Getting Things Done* (2002), was not a manifesto (as the title might suggest) for supporters of capital punishment. It was, rather, an attempt to show managers and strategists how to translate ideas, especially about growth, into action. Execution may be an art, but it depends a lot on discipline and action. The book is, at heart, an operations manifesto, a point Bossidy drove home by commenting: "Many people regard execution as detail work that's beneath the dignity of a business leader. That is wrong. To the contrary, it's a leader's most important job. Problems can fester when there is too little action [or] when the wrong person is in the wrong job for too long."

His next collaboration with Ram Charan, *Confronting Reality: Doing What Matters to Get Things Right* (2004), wears its heart on its dust jacket. The business world is changing for everyone. It is tough to survive, he asserts, but the only way to survive is to wake up and become more savvy. The best way to do this is by asking a lot of deep questions. The first set of questions concerns your company's position in its particular sector:

+   Has the way money is made in your business sector or industry changed?
+   Who is winning? Who isn't? Why?
+   If you're among the winners, how do you stay there?
+   If you belong – perhaps not to the losers, but to the "non-winners" – what should you do to improve things?

Other questions involve inquiry into the fundamentals of the business sector or industry itself:

+   Can you see growth ahead? How do you get there? By beating the competition or by doing things better or differently?
+   If you cannot see growth, what should you do?
+   Is your organization fleet-footed enough to exploit growth opportunities when they emerge, possibly in unsuspecting places?

There are also questions tied to issues specific to industry and technology:

+   Are supply and demand in balance?
+   Are your products being commoditized?
+   Are they structurally defective or heading for obsolescence?
+   Where do you stand vis-à-vis the competition?
+   How does your stuff look in the eyes of the customer?

+ Where is the technology going? Can you foresee any big breakthroughs down the line?
+ What about your internal talent? Does it shape up to the competition?
+ Do you have legacy costs from the past that may sabotage your competitive advantage?

Bossidy believes the answers to these questions are rarely to be found within the organization itself. Insiders (when asked to address such questions) too often have a built-in distortion filter. They often can't come to terms with reality.

However, Bossidy and Charan do more than just ask questions in the book. They provide a new business point of view that is "robust and reality-based," one that takes a holistic view of the business environment. Their proposals are supplemented by examples from across the corporate world. The model for the kind of business strategy they suggest involves examination of two factors and the utilization of a third:

+ External realities: financial history, the broader business environment, root cause analysis (a warts-and-all examination of what went wrong, what went right, and why)
+ Internal activities and standard functions: strategy, operations and tactics, structures, recruitment, and other related issues
+ Financially objective metrics (which must underpin the model): operating margins, cash flow, and return-on-investment

Essential reading

http://www.honeywell.com/execution/bio_larry.html
Execution: The Art of Getting Things Done (Crown, 2002) (with Ram Charan and Charles Burck)
Confronting Reality: Doing What Matters to Get Things Right (Crown, 2004) (with Ram Charan)

RICHARD BRANSON
Chairman of the Virgin Group
(2005 Ranking: 11)

....

In his youth Richard Branson (born 1950) combined a traditional upbringing with a rebellious streak. While at Stowe (a "minor" English public school), he set up *Student* magazine followed by a student advisory service a year later. In 1970 he founded a discount mail-order record company with his friend Nik Powell and established a record shop in London's Oxford Street. He also launched a recording label called Virgin. Among the label's early signings was Mike Oldfield, whose album *Tubular Bells* was a great hit. Virgin also signed up the Sex Pistols when nobody else would. Virgin developed interests in music publishing and recording studios, eventually becoming the Virgin Music Group. Branson sold this in 1992 to Thorn EMI. He re-established his presence in the recording world in 1996 with the launch of V2 Records, whose stable includes bands like Stereophonics.

The Virgin Group has expanded phenomenally, embracing nearly 200 companies. It is involved in hotels, fitness clubs (Virgin Active), books, software production, and film and video editing. There are also Virgin Holidays and Virgin Credit Cards.

One of the best-known companies has been Virgin Atlantic Airlines, founded in 1984. This is a long-haul transatlantic carrier, aiming to provide value-for-money flights on transatlantic routes. There are now cut-price airlines, such as Virgin Blue in Australia. In the U.K. there is Virgin Trains.

However, for Branson, Earth is not enough. One of his projects is Virgin Galactic, which plans to offer affordable space travel for those wanting to leave the world behind for a few hours. It is certain that its first mission will carry his beaming, bearded, slightly disheveled face.

Branson is always eager for a new challenge in business. As there are few interesting ones that he hasn't tried, he is even open to offers from visitors to the virgin.com site. He claims that each new business adventure is the product of instinct, not of financial and strategic planning. He is rather contemptuous of business theorizing: "I never get the accountants in before I start up a business. It's done on gut feeling …"

Branson has become the most successful brand-master of our time. At the center of it all is the core brand, Virgin. This spreads its tentacles in the directions Branson desires in a process often called "virginization." The Virgin brand transcends products and industries in a way that defies business sense about brand dilution. Branson once said, "I want Virgin to be as well known around the world as Coca-Cola." Many feel he has succeeded, though others say he had a head start with the name.

He assigns Virgin's success to:

+ Value for money
+ Quality
+ Reliability
+ Innovation
+ Fun

He is not shy of publicity, something he has gained in his various "record-breaking" balloon and boat trips. He wanted to be the first person to go around the world in a hot-air balloon, but Steve Fossett beat him to it. Whenever he tries to break a new record, the vehicle is splattered with the Virgin logo, giving immense and immeasurable brand placement.

The Virgin brand is big. The Virgin brand is also Richard Branson. He is careful about the messages that both send out, knowing how one influences the other. He also knows the value of always appearing to be "cool."

For Branson life and business are fun: "Sometimes I do wake up in the mornings and feel like I've just had the most incredible dream. I've just dreamt my life."

He is also heavily involved in charity work. Sometimes this has been controversial, such as his sponsorship of Parents Against Tobacco. He is also a trustee of the Healthcare Foundation in the U.K. For his work in the world of business, he was knighted in 2000; but he nonetheless prefers to be called, simply, Richard.

The activities of Virgin/Richard Branson are so visible everywhere that there apparently is not a need for him to put his ideas on success and entrepreneurship into writing. There are Virgin Business Guides on various topics, such as *Do Something Different: Proven Marketing Techniques to Transform your Business* (2001), not written by Branson himself (though usually carrying a foreword by him).

Some of his business philosophy can be found in his autobiography *Losing My Virginity* (1999). This gives insights into a lot of his business activity in the 1970s and '80s.

Essential reading

http://www.virgin.com/aboutvirgin/allaboutvirgin/whosrichardbranson/
    default.asp
Losing My Virginity (Crown, 1999)

JAMES CHAMPY AND MICHAEL HAMMER

Consultants (2005 Ranking: 44)

Jim Champy was born in Lawrence, Massachusetts. He trained as a civil engineer at MIT, though he had initially wanted to become an architect. He subsequently trained as an attorney. After a spell running the family construction firm, he co-founded Index, a successful management consultancy that became CSC Index. He later joined Perot Systems, where he is chairman of consulting.

Michael Hammer also studied engineering at MIT, gaining a Ph.D. For many years he was a Professor of Computing Science there before founding Hammer & Company, a management education business.

In the 1980s both men worked on ways of applying the greater availability of computers to everyday business processes. Many companies feared that the mere computerization of activities was not leading to greater efficiencies in terms of time or money saved. Computerization could deliver these, they said, but only if it formed part of extensive changes in company practice. Existing functional divisions were often obstructive and wasteful. "We've had the same answer for 40 years, but the questions have changed." Companies often needed to be atomized (figuratively) and put back together, or rather, put back together better. They termed the changes that would have to be made as corporate or business process reengineering (BPR). Thanks to their best-selling book *Reengineering The Corporation* (1993), reengineering entered the management lexicon.

When management thinkers use emotive words like "revolution," they see a need to give bangs for bucks. There is no such thing as a quiet revolution. There has to be blood on the floor. Hammer gave some indication of what was needed in a *Harvard Business Review* article called "Reengineering Work: Don't Automate, Obliterate."

BPR started (usually aided by consultants) with an analysis of a company's core strengths and the factors that made it better than its competitors. The second step isolated what contributed to this competitive advantage. Champy and Hammer termed this business value analysis (BVA). This had to get to the heart of where the competitive advantage lay. It had to distinguish between processes and activities that contributed, and those that were secondary or maybe contributed nothing at all. The final stage was the implementation of new structures. These were dedicated to the development of competitive processes adding business value. These often took the form of cross-functional, self-managing teams. This promised efficiency and more growth. It also seemed to spell the demolition of functional chimneys in firms, and their replacement by a leaner, flatter structure. This would have better communication at a horizontal level between teams than would a top-down approach.

Much of BPR's initial take-up stemmed from frustration at continuing bureaucracy and top-heavy management structures that thumbed their noses at the march of technology. Many were fed up with the persistence of quasi-military hierarchies and departments acting like states within a state. Yet little in reengineering was new.

Many companies reaped the benefits of the whirlwind of greater efficiency and more effective use of technology. Kodak cut response times between order and product delivery by half. Hammer wanted to go further than just business processes. Reengineering was the work of angels, he once said. It was tackling the great scandal of our time – inefficiency. Fix that and everything would fall into place.

At the same time, these companies got smaller and many people were trash-canned. Those left behind had to work harder or in different ways. So BPR was derided as verbose window-dressing accompanying downsizing. Others saw it as a return of the nefarious influence of Frederick Taylor's scientific management. Champy's firm, CSC Index, renamed their offering business process improvement (BPI) which offered much of the gain of BPR with less of the pain.

Champy was also sensitive to another big weakness in the application of BPR. Some managers were very keen for other parts of the organization to be reengineered, so long as they were left untouched. In his book *Reengineering Management* (1995) he wrote, "If their jobs and styles are left largely intact, managers will eventually undermine the very structures of their rebuilt organizations."

Champy has since written *The Arc of Ambition* (2001). This looks at visionaries who were considered insane through much of their lifetime. Their visions were later carried to fruition by capitalists and consolidators, and their memories were rehabilitated.

Essential reading

(Champy) http://www.jimchampy.com/

(Hammer) http://www.hammerandco.com/about.asp

Reengineering the Corporation: A Manifesto for Business Revolution (Harper Collins, 1993) (Champy and Hammer)

Reengineering Management: The Mandate for New Leadership (Diane Publishing, 1995) (Champy)

Fast Forward: The Best Ideas on Managing Business Change (Harvard Business School Press, 1996) (Champy with Nitin Nohria)

The Arc of Ambition: Defining the Leadership Journey (Perseus, 2001) (Champy with Nitin Nohria)

X-Engineering the Corporation: Reinventing Your Business in the Digital Age (Warner, 2002) (Champy)

Beyond Reengineering: How the Process-centered Organization Is Changing Our Work and Our Lives (Collins, 1998) (Hammer)

RAM CHARAN

Consultant and Executive Coach

(2005 Ranking: 24)

Ram Charan was born and brought up in a small town in rural northern India. After earning an M.B.A. from the Harvard Business School, he worked on the HBS faculty for some years. He then concentrated on his own consultancy and mentoring work. Although he is based in Dallas, Texas, he spends little time there.

He has coached CEOs of numerous Fortune 100 companies, including GE's Jack Welch. However, Charan has never been an *éminence grise* working behind the corporate throne. His coaching has been accompanied by a steady stream of publications available in various formats.

Like many top-notch Indian management thinkers, his upbringing had a decisive influence on him. He was born into a large family running a small shoe shop. Everyone had to do their bit to keep the business going – making, selling and repairing shoes. If it failed, there awaited misery, starvation, and maybe death. The shoe business helped pay for his education. It also taught him the importance of business acumen – something that unites the successful Indian fruit seller and the good CEO. Both know the universal laws of business – cash flow, margin, high velocity, and healthy growth.

His messages for CEOs are shaped by the ups and downs in business activity. Downturns can be times of opportunity, when it is important to retain a proactive approach, never losing any opportunity to innovate and communicate with customers and suppliers. Companies must lower their bottom lines before the competition does. It is easy to imagine Ram Charan as a boxing coach. His boxer (executive) is behind on points, and between rounds he tells him, "You're not going to win the fight sitting in the corner – go out there and fight."

As he has coached, he has observed. He has attempted to provide some answers as to why the management soufflé often falls flat even though all of the recipe's ingredients are there in the right quantities. The story of corporate America (and corporate anywhere) is littered with people who, after a sequence of bad results, get reassigned to the trashcan. These people worked hard to get to where they were. They were successful, often spectacularly so. They were intelligent too, and they often had lots of vision. However, vision and inspiration are never enough. Ask any of the world's top golfers. They tee off with the vision of breaking the course record but, after a couple of visits to the paddling pool and a few rolls in the heavy rough, they end up missing the cut. Vision and intelligence fall flat if the execution and the follow-through are flawed. Effective execution demands having the right people in the right jobs: people who know what is expected of them. The people at the top need business acumen; failure results from having someone with the wrong type of good reputation, say as a dealmaker or someone unable to set priorities. He never puts CEO failure down to a pithy sound bite. Much of the problem stems from lack of "emotional strength."

Ram Charan pursued his own follow-through strategy with his book, co-authored with Larry Bossidy, entitled *Execution* (2002). The successful company has good strong leadership, but leadership should be nurtured throughout the organization. There should be a leadership pipeline within the organization. There must also be good communications. The CEO is dependent on having a good and efficient board of directors. Everyone within the organization has a vital role to play. They should all feel valued, but they should never be allowed to forget their interdependence. Everyone should be aware of the big picture and their part in it. This prompted him to write *What The CEO Wants You to Know* (2001). This was an unfortunate title, as it invited "alternatives" such as *What the CEO Doesn't Want You (or anyone else) to Know* (a thicker tome, no doubt). A more appropriate title would have been *What Everyone in Business Should Know*.

Ram Charan believes in an active, hands-on approach to management, and is an advocate of management by walking around for the digital age. He cites Wal-Mart founder Sam Walton as a good role model. The customer should never be forgotten. Many firms have nose-dived by losing touch with what their customers want or by being too arrogant to ask.

Essential reading

http://www.randomhouse.com/crown/catalog/results.pperl?authorid=4694

Every Business Is a Growth Business (Wiley, 1999) (with Noel Tichy)

What the CEO Wants You to Know: The Little Book of Big Business (Crown, 2001)

Execution: The Discipline of Getting Things Done (Crown, 2002) (with Larry Bossidy *et al.*)

Confronting Reality: Master the New Model for Success (Crown, 2004) (with Larry Bossidy *et al.*)

CLAYTON CHRISTENSEN

Educator (2005 Ranking: 21)

Clayton Christensen is Robert and Jane Cizik Professor of Business Administration at the Harvard Business School.

After graduating in economics from Brigham Young University in his native Utah, he went to Oxford as a Rhodes Scholar, earning an M.Phil. in Applied Econometrics. He returned to the U.S. and to the Harvard Business School, gaining an M.B.A. and D.B.A. He worked as a consultant and project manager with the Boston Consulting Group before establishing Ceramics Process Systems Corporation (CPS), a high-technology manufacturing company. In 1992 he returned to Harvard and joined the Business School faculty.

He is best known to a wider audience as the author of the award-winning *The Innovator's Dilemma* (1997). The technological or digital writing was on the wall. Technological innovation was no longer an option but an imperative for survival. Many companies could point to large profits from innovation. He gave examples of companies with products that changed the competitive playing field – the Honda Supercub, the Intel 8088 processor. They didn't have grand business plans for these products. They went in at the low end of the market pool and thereby gained entrance to the bigger pool. They eventually displaced the competition from the high end of the market. Christensen characterizes these products as disruptive technologies.

So the message was stark: innovate or die. Well, it wasn't that simple. Innovation could be tricky. Christensen highlighted that many large existing companies found real innovation not only challenging but also difficult. Innovation was completely different from mere improvement – fine-tuning or tinkering with existing systems and structures. However, many firms had invested a lot in these existing structures and were squeamish about writing them off. They paid lip service to innovation, but anything that might upset established certainties was likely to be dismissed. This often blinds companies to the possibilities and profitability offered by innovation.

Innovating companies need creative people. This causes its own set of problems for both established companies and start-ups. The brightest and best may not want to be truly creative (and produce breakthrough solutions) for someone else. They may prefer to wait until they can go it alone and reap their own harvest. Retaining free spirits within the corporate structure provides another dilemma for those wanting to innovate. Some have responded in novel ways by establishing in-house incubators or promoting the establishment of spin-out companies.

Christensen earned a reputation as the guru of disruption, a late twentieth-century equivalent of the "Lord of Misrule" in medieval carnival. He has since moved on to a discussion of strategy in the age of innovation. He defines strategy, perhaps a little narrowly for some, as being about creating competitive advantage. Strategists seem stuck in a time warp of the present. They laud successful companies like Dell and Cisco Systems. They preach the mantra "if it's good for Cisco, chances are it's good for everyone." They don't realize the success of these companies is specific to the present. There is no guarantee that they or their models will be profitable in twenty, ten, even five years' time. History teaches the transience of corporate success. Models that were successful once, such as IBM's vertical integration in the 1970s, wouldn't work now. Instead of preaching emulation, strategists should identify what allows the Dells and the Cisco Systems to succeed. They should stop identifying *what* works and begin to ask (and answer) *why* it works.

This is important throughout the corporate world. Many mid-sized pharmaceutical firms are merging, hoping to counter prohibitive costs associated with the research, development, and testing of new drugs. However, the advent of new forms of biotechnology, especially connected with exploitation of the human genome, may reduce these costs. The quest for competitive advantage can be frustrating: it is like playing hide-and-seek in thick fog. As competitors try to level the playing field the competitive advantage sought (and maybe briefly realized) disappears. So is the pursuit of competitive advantage worth the candle? Christensen's answer is a most definite yes. Strategists can play along too. They must develop a much deeper, almost three-dimensional comprehension of "the processes of competition and progress and of the factors that undergird each advantage."

Essential reading

http://www.claytonchristensen.com

The Innovator's Dilemma: When New Technologies Cause Great Firms to Fail (Harvard Business School Press, 1997)

"The Past and Future of Competitive Advantage," *Sloan Management Review,* Vol. 42 No. 2 (Winter 2001)

The Innovator's Solution: Creating and Sustaining Successful Growth (Harvard Business School Press, 2003) (with Michael Raynor)

JAMES C. COLLINS

Consultant and Climber

(2005 Ranking: 6)

Jim Collins was born in Boulder, Colorado. He studied business at Stanford and stayed on at the faculty after graduating. Having taught at Stanford for seven years, he returned to his hometown to establish what he called a business research laboratory. Here he has become "a self-employed professor who endowed his own chair and granted himself tenure." His laboratory examines business issues and structures from a statistical standpoint. "Others like opinions," says Collins. "I prefer data." His desire for certainty contrasts with his out of work enthusiasm for the uncertainty of mountaineering.

His research work has involved looking at large numbers of companies to find out what makes some good, others great, and others still downright awful. This involves a probe into how each company is managed and the role of its CEO. His research has resulted in four books, including *Good to Great* (2001).

Good to Great emerged from a simple question: Can a good company become a great company? Collins and his researchers' answer was yes – but it was not easy. Collins started with a data set of over 1,000 companies but whittled this down to 11 that had consistently outperformed their rivals. These companies had things in common, but not what conventional B-school wisdom said they should have. It was easier to see what they lacked: high-profile CEOs, cutting-edge technology implementation, a business strategy or even change management. What Collins did find among the eleven was a common corporate culture that was big on the very outdated concept of discipline. This was not the discipline of the martinet, but the good type – self-discipline. The companies rewarded self-disciplined people who thought in a self-disciplined way.

However, the difference between the good and the great was also attributable to different *types* of leadership. Collins says he was initially a leadership skeptic: it was too simple to pin great success or grim failure on the lapels of a leader. However, this is what his data was telling him. On further investigation he identified two levels of leadership – level 5 (the great) and level 4 (the good).

None of this is cast in stone, and a level 4 leader can improve. Collins cites Lou Gerstner as an example: a level 4 manager at R.J. Reynolds who became a level 5 manager at IBM – though not immediately. Level 5 people have an almost heroic commitment to the company and its mission. The company gets all their emotions – there is no room or energy for self-promotion. This does not mean that level 5 managers are shrinking violets. They simply put the company before, well, everything – family, friends, and probably their health. But they are never alone. They should have a good team around them. This is their responsibility. Part of the mettle of the level 5 manager is deciding who should be on the bus and where they should sit.

There are other qualities that set the great apart from the good. These include the performance of their companies, which can be measured by financial results. Collins is a keen believer in assessing success through the company's stock price. This indicates a preference for publicly quoted companies.

A level 5 leader must also have the respect of other business and industry players, such as competitors. (Respect, of course, has nothing to do with liking.) They should have an impact on their company – maybe their industry – that outlasts them.

Collins' researchers also looked at the identity of CEOs. Those companies that chose their chief executives from inside the organization did better than those preferring outsiders. He suggested that outsiders are ignorant of the company they are entering at the top, having no gestation or apprenticeship period. He also suggested that outsiders lacked the capacity for commitment to a long-term relationship along with its necessary sacrifices.

Good CEOs should be neither too humble nor too proud. They should not be too charismatic. They should ideally stay in the job for a minimum of seven years, as it is not possible to have any impact in a lesser time.

In his earlier book, *Built to Last* (1995), Collins (along with Jerry Porras) focused on visionary companies, looking in depth at 18 out of an original list of many dozens. These 18 companies are united by widespread brand recognition, are world-famous, but have been in business for more than 50 years. It was their "staying power" that fascinated Collins and Porras; their book thus tried to dissect and profile true visionary leadership.

Collins' research stems from the corporate arena, but he reminds his readers that the lessons he puts forward are equally applicable in the non-corporate arena.

Essential reading

http://www.jimcollins.com

Beyond Entrepreneurship: Turning Your Business into an Enduring Great Company (Prentice Hall, 1995) (with William Lazier)

Built to Last: Successful Habits of Visionary Companies (Collins, 1995) (with Jerry Porras)

Good to Great: Why Some Companies Make the Leap ... and Others Don't (Collins, 2001)

STEPHEN COVEY

Self-helper (2005 Ranking: 18)

Stephen R. Covey (born 1932) is co-founder and co-chairman of Franklin Covey, "the largest management and leadership development organization in the world."

He earned an M.B.A. at Harvard and his doctorate from Brigham Young University. He worked on the faculty there as a professor of Business Management and Organizational Behavior.

He is an author, speaker, and success coach. He wrote the best-selling *The 7 Habits of Highly Effective People* (1989). It stayed on the *New York Times* best-seller chart for an amazing 260 weeks and is estimated to have sold in excess of 12 million copies in 32 languages. It was not surprising that it sold so well since its title alone promised success: it was similar to The Ten Commandments. Its quasi-religious message has been backed up by other books by Covey, such as *Daily Reflections for Highly Reflective People: Living the 7 Habits Every Day* (1994). This has the resonance of a call to daily prayer.

Rather than stick with words, he has sought to teach and to coach as well. He established the very successful Covey Leadership Center near Salt Lake City. In 1997 it merged with training company Franklin Quest to form Franklin Covey. The company runs seminars, operates a speaker's bureau, and produces audiocassettes, videos, and software. It also is heavily involved in retailing its particular success messages and products, with 110 stores in the U.S., online shopping facilities, 4,300 employees, and a turnover in excess of $500 million.

Covey is not afraid to boast. Franklin Covey attracts high-caliber people to its courses and other offerings. They include people from 90 of the Fortune

100 companies and three-quarters from the Fortune 500 list. It operates in over 90 countries.

So what is the Stephen Covey philosophy? Don't mention big foreign words like that! It is a truism to say that it is all just common sense. There is no theory. A lot of use is made of homespun stuff, the type of thing grandpa and grandma told their kids. The seven habits are:

1 Be proactive
2 Begin with an end in mind
3 Put first things first
4 Think win/win
5 Seek first to understand, then to be understood
6 Synergize: the whole is always greater than the sum of its parts
7 Sharpen the saw – keep improving and innovating

But Covey admits that he is no guru: "I did not invent the seven habits, they are universal principles, and most of what I wrote about is just common sense. I am embarrassed when people talk about the *Covey* Habits."

Covey is a devout Mormon for whom material success is to be neither feared nor shunned. It has been said that much of his thinking is really spiritual messages dressed in pinstripes.

He has been awarded numerous distinctions. Covey was awarded the Thomas More College Medallion for continuing service to humanity as well as the Sikh's 1998 International Man of Peace Award.

Since *The 7 Habits* he has written *The 8th Habit* (2004). This recognizes even more the role of the Divine in corporate affairs: "The more we use and magnify our present talents, the more talents we are given and the greater our capacity becomes."

All humans can tap into a reservoir of unexplored potential. But to do this involves finding a balance of four human attributes: talent, need, passion, and conscience.

Naturally Dr. Covey is a committed family man. One of his titles is *The 7 Habits of Highly Effective Families* (1999). He has inculcated the values he holds dear into his children. His son Sean has even written a book called *The 7 Habits of Highly Effective Teens* (1998), followed up a year later by *Daily Reflections for Highly Effective Teens* (1999).

Essential reading

http://www.stephencovey.com
The 7 Habits of Highly Effective People (Free Press, 1989)
The 8th Habit: From Effectiveness to Greatness (Free Press, 2004)

EDWARD DE BONO
Lateral Thinker (2005 Ranking: 20)

Edward de Bono (born 1933) studied medicine in his native Malta, before going to Oxford as a Rhodes Scholar. There he gained a Ph.D. in psychology and physiology. He has lectured at many of the world's leading universities. He has also consulted to numerous international corporations, many of which use his works as part of their training programs. His teaching methods have been used in many schools, from primary to adult education. He has received several awards and honorary degrees. He has even had a minor asteroid named in his honor.

De Bono has dedicated his life to researching thought and how humans perceive and make sense of information. The role of creativity is central. He has sought a wide audience for his views, although some psychologists have dismissed this as populism. In *The Mechanisms of Mind* (1969) he demonstrated that our perceptions are based on asymmetric pattern formations in the brain: "Perception is real even when it is not reality."

This led to the development of his theory of "lateral thinking," outlined in works like *Lateral Thinking* (1977) and *Teach Yourself to Think* (1995).

In a stable world, human beings apply standard solutions to standard situations based on tools like analysis, judgment and argument. However, in a world, or any situation, which is in flux, these standard formulae are inapplicable. A common response to a problem has been to identify the cause and remove it. But this is no longer sufficient. Traditional thinking is all about what is. Future thinking will need to be about what can be. We may need to solve problems not by removing the cause but by designing the way forward even if the cause remains in place. Creativity is often called for. De Bono provides new tools to help people create solutions to new problems: "If you do not design the future, someone or something else will design it for you."

Six Thinking Hats (1985) undermines the importance assigned to argument as a means of problem solving. De Bono considers it a wasteful form of effort. It is accompanied by the squandering of intellectual energy and the nurturing of egos. The Six Hats concept emerged from a study of how the chemistry of the brain changes with different types of thought. Meetings are unproductive because of muddled thinking. He sets out a schema like a child's game, with six colored hats, each associated with a necessary thought process.

In *I Am Right, You Are Wrong* (1990) he assesses the world's inability to deal with its many problems because it is reliant on old methods of analysis. Not only are these ineffective at providing solutions, they are also dangerous. They generate polarized self-righteousness, as expressed in the title. This leads to creativity-killing defensiveness.

In *New Thinking for the New Millennium* (2000) De Bono describes how the technological advances of the second millennium have not been matched by changes in the way we think. He also argues for some new approaches to the use of language, implying that human beings can happily deal with a higher order of communication.

De Bono has written for many different audiences: parents, teachers, designers, and especially people in business. One of his most recent contributions has been *The Six Value Medals* (2005). Success no longer comes through analyzing the past but in creating and molding the future. Values persist in the midst of this contemporary maelstrom: "Effectiveness without values is a tool without a purpose." Disputes and controversies develop because values clash. Each party often believes the only way is to pursue their values to the end in a zero-sum game – we win and you lose. The way ahead is for everyone involved in a problem – be they CEOs or people lower down the organization – to find creative solutions. Values will still come into conflict, but resolving the conflict can create new opportunities. De Bono highlights the different types of values in an organization. These may be:

+ Human
+ Cultural
+ Organizational
+ Perceptional

He has developed a scoring system to measure whether the various values are strong, sound, weak, or remote.

De Bono claims his theories have been used by companies and governments around the world. He also claims that he has received reports of from 20 to 90 percent less time being spent in meetings by people who have followed his methods.

Essential reading

http://www.edwdebono.com
Lateral Thinking: A Textbook of Creativity (Harper & Row, 1977)
Six Thinking Hats (Viking, 1985)
I Am Right, You Are Wrong: From This to the New Renaissance, from Rock Logic to Water Logic (Viking, 1990)
New Thinking for the New Millennium (New Millennium Entertainment, 2000)
The Six Value Medals (Ebury Press, 2005)

MICHAEL DELL

Chairman and Founder of Dell Computers

(2005 Ranking: 29)

Michael Dell (born 1965) is chairman of Dell Inc. He was born in Houston, Texas. His mother was a stockbroker. He had an early interest in computers. He received an Apple II computer for his fifteenth birthday, which, to the horror of his parents, he proceeded to take apart. He soon switched from Apple to the newly arrived IBM PCs, customizing them and adding additional features. Another early interest was making money, and he found that he could combine the two successfully. His parents had a medical career in mind for young Michael. He went to the University of Texas at Austin, but he pursued his ever more lucrative business from his dormitory room.

The concept of customized PCs gave him a business idea. Customers could get their very own machine or system, catering to their needs with no unnecessary or underused extras. If computers could be built to order, it would mean the middleman in his various retail guises could be cut out of the deal. This would have enormous cost benefits for the end consumer. There would be other benefits too. Inventory could be kept low if the assembly was carried out to order on a just-in-time basis. The customer would still get a high-quality product for which they were willing to pay, so cash flow would not be a problem. High velocity would mean substantial returns, even with low margins. This direct method had been tried before, as Dell admits, but only to cater to large business accounts.

Rather than wait for someone else to develop the idea, Dell founded Dell Computer with around $1,000. The rest, they say, is ... In his book *Direct from Dell* (1999), he stated his belief that having limited financial resources at the start can help a business. In the early days Dell Computer had annual sales of $6 million, not bad at the time; but this figure was in excess of $41 billion in 2004. It employs over 57,000 "team members" worldwide.

Dell subsequently dropped out of college. His company started making its own computers. It could offer next-day delivery in the U.S. In 1987 Dell went international, opening a subsidiary in the U.K. It has since established manufacturing facilities throughout the world. The company was included in the Fortune 500 in 1992. Its CEO was only 27, and in the following year the company was among the top five computer systems providers worldwide. By 2001 it was the number one computer systems provider by market share.

The advent of the Internet was embraced eagerly by Dell. In 1995 ordering online was introduced. Five years later daily sales via the Internet were reckoned to be worth $50 million.

In 1988 Dell Computer went public. It has been an investor's darling, with a nearly 50,000 percent increase in value during the 1990s. The new century has seen a decline in PC sales and margins worldwide, not just for Dell. The company has responded by putting more emphasis on servers, workstations, and computer technology services. It has also entered the consumer electronics industry. To reflect this change in emphasis the company dropped "computer" from its name to become plain Dell Inc.

For Michael Dell, customers are important. He has claimed that he spends 40 percent of his time with customers. A lot of the rest goes into designing improved ways to listen to customers. It is more important for a company to study its customers than its competitors, he advocates.

Dell has created a revolutionary business model. In 1999 he put many of his thoughts about business into a book – *Direct from Dell*. These included his belief in vertical integration in the computer industry. He also gave tips on how to exploit the competition's weakness by exposing its greatest strength. He also stressed the value of communications: between the company, its staff, its suppliers, and naturally its customers. An important part of communicating is listening and acting quickly. Errors are thus kept to a minimum.

Dell Inc. has also demonstrated a commitment to the environment. In 2003 it launched Dell Recycle, an initiative to help users of any computer equipment, regardless of manufacturer, either to recycle it or to donate it to charity.

Essential reading

http://www1.us.dell.com/content/topics/global.aspx/corp/biographies/
en/msd_index?c=us&l=en&s=corp

Direct From Dell: Strategies that Revolutionized an Industry (Collins, 1999)
(with Catherine Fredman)

PATRICK DIXON
Consultant (2005 Ranking: 17)

Dr. Patrick Dixon is the chairman of Global Change Ltd., a consulting and forecasting group. He is also a fellow of the Centre for Management Development at London Business School.

He is a rare bird among the ranks of management thinkers: he is a physician. He has achieved fame by taking the pulse of today and attempting to diagnose the shape of tomorrow.

He is a graduate of King's College Cambridge and Charing Cross Hospital medical school. In his years as a medical practitioner he combined care for those suffering from cancer and AIDS with an interest in information technology. His first book, *The Truth About AIDS* (1988), coincided with the foundation of ACET, an international alliance that aimed to educate people about the disease and treat victims.

The success of this book prompted Dixon to produce more volumes on topical issues. This coincided with invitations from multinationals to lecture on a wide range of issues, from corporate governance to the need for better market research.

Some of his books reflected his interests in Christianity and social action, such as *Signs of Revival* (1994) and *Cyberchurch* (1997). His book *The Rising Price of Love* (1995) aimed to show, from a Christian perspective, that "free love" came at a cost.

In *Futurewise* (1998) Dixon examines six trends that he identifies as shaping the modern world. The world of the future will be:

+ Fast: speed, in transport, communications, delivery – in everything – will be imperative
+ Urban: more people will end up living in cities as they grow
+ Tribal: cultural and religious conflicts show no sign of disappearing
+ Universal: globalization is creating a global marketplace
+ Radical: there is a reaction (for good or bad) against much of twentieth-century morality
+ Ethical: a new morality is needed and can be discerned

Some of these trends will conflict; others will resolve themselves. The book also contains 500 "key expectations."

The growing power and reach of the Internet is a topic of great interest to Dixon, and he has used the Internet himself to spread his message. His website contains the full text of six of his books for free download, as well as other materials such as videos. In many ways this is an application of direct methods of sales. He feels pleasure in giving away his intellectual capital. He sees free availability of ideas as an essential element of the twenty-first-century world. "The real added-value … is knowing exactly how to *apply* ideas to build a better kind of future for your own business, yourself, family, community and wider world." He also operates a Web TV station and has a radio and recording studio at his home.

His most recent book, *Building a Better Business* (2005), is not just another self-help manual. Dixon has a philosophical and spiritual message. Marketing, management, and financial issues are still important. The aim of the better business, though, is not just to make a profit but to attain and consolidate a better life and better world. This involves solving long-term dilemmas like the work/life balance. He sees businesses, large and small, as facing a motivational crisis. To overcome this they have to "rediscover their real purpose." He gives a five-point guide to how to do this:

+ Reconnect with your true purpose
+ Focus far more on the good the company does
+ Take a wider view – what else can the company do?
+ Connect with the passions of your staff and customers
+ Put your money where your mouth is

Essential reading

http://www.globalchange.com/cv.htm
Futurewise: Six Faces of Global Change (Harper Collins, 1998)
Building a Better Business (Profile, 2005)

LEIF EDVINSSON

Consultant (2005 Ranking: 43)

Leif Edvinsson (born 1946) is the Professor of Intellectual Capital at Lund University, Sweden, the first to hold this academic title. He is also the CEO of Universal Networking Intellectual Capital. He received an M.B.A. from the University of California and then returned to the Swedish business world, where he pursued his skills in training and consulting. He was vice president for training and development at S-E Bank; he also served as chairman of Consultus AB, a Stockholm-based consulting company. Edvinsson was subsequently appointed the first director of intellectual capital at Skandia Insurance Company Ltd. He serves as a member of the Board of Trustees for England's Brain Trust, which in 1998 awarded him the "Brain of the Year." Most recently, he was listed among the top 20 list of Most Admired Knowledge Leaders In The World.

Most people in business know or should know about capital. In general, the term refers to hard resources, such as monetary wealth or inventories. Many non-business thinkers, like Karl Marx, have also written on the topic using different points of view. In the 1980s, many writers focused on social capital. The following decade saw the birth and nurturing of the concept of intellectual capital, the collective brainpower of an organization.

Intellectual capital is the intangible learning or accumulated knowledge that helps an enterprise do what it does, the "capital" that employees bring home with them in their heads every evening. It is always an intangible asset – that's a given. So, before it can be accepted as real capital, a valuation has to be put on it. While at Skandia, Edvinsson produced the first Intellectual Capital Annual Report. This led in 1997 to the publication of *Intellectual*

Capital: Realizing Your Company's True Value by Finding its Hidden Brainpower. This book provided the means by which intellectual capital could be calculated into hard numbers. Edvinsson and co-author Michael Malone predicted that many firms would eventually find (via such calculations) that their intellectual assets outstripped their physical assets!

However, intellectual capital deals with far more than mere quantification. Edvinsson believes that it represents the start of a compounded valuation. An organization's intellectual capital, its collective brainpower, can be multiplied by its structural capital – the elements contained among customers, databases, structures, processes, and brands – thus creating, in essence, an intellectual capital multiplier.

Edvinsson believes that corporate leadership should be less preoccupied with items like standard budgets and more open to experimenting, even prototyping, new techniques that involve intangible values such as the rise or fall of a company's intellectual capital. Too much stress has historically been set on traditional measuring methods, he feels. Cost accounting often gives a distorted, if not misleading, picture of the fortunes or failings of a company. It is hard to assess intellectual capital, which is why the subject needs rigorous study. For example, the loss of a key technician may even show up as a gain, depending on how it is evaluated! Edvinsson uses a nautical analogy to express this. Traditional methods provide the equivalent of latitude readings. Intellectual capital assessment gives a more complete picture. It is "corporate longitude." Thus, the assessment of intellectual capital and the use of mind-compass methodology are outlined in his book, *Corporate Longitude* (2002).

One of the new roles of leadership is to protect and nurture intellectual capital. Because this kind of capital is human, it can be easily destroyed or rendered less valuable by bad management practices. This can happen when the working environment is human-averse, even outright hostile to humans. Factors that can impact intellectual capital negatively are excessively long work hours or intensely stressful work tasks. Edvinsson argues that, when such issues are uncovered, managerial defensiveness can be harmful. Instead, transparency must be the rule. Organizations should welcome new per-spectives and non-traditional solutions. These can include using part-time workers to relieve stress levels, as well as utilizing the skills of retired people. Managers, he believes, should often adopt a more federal structure with less emphasis on hierarchical command and control. He has even spoken of elimi-nating traditional offices and replacing them with "knowledge cafes." The intellectually capitalized world may be uncomfortable for some, but the gains outweigh any losses, he asserts. Thus, discomfort could, in the end, be healthy for all.

Accepting the existence and realizing the potential of intellectual capi-tal is not just an issue for commercial organizations. Nations, regions, and cities also have intellectual capital. Some utilize their human capital better than others. Obviously an important way of utilizing brainpower is through education, but the education system often needs to be re-thought so that it produces optimum results for all. For example, Edvinsson talks about intel-lectual tourism, attracting visitors to come to centers of educational and technical excellence in order to learn and acquire knowledge. "The intellec-tual wealth of nations," says Edvinsson, "is the new wealth of nations."

Essential reading

http://www.unic.net/
Intellectual Capital: Realizing Your Company's True Value by Finding its Hidden Brainpower (Harper Business, 1997) (with Michael S. Malone)
Intellectual Capital: Navigating in the New Business Landscape (New York University Press, 1998) (with Goran Roos, Nicola Carlo Dragonetti and Johan Roos)
Corporate Longitude: Discover Your True Position in the Knowledge Economy (Financial Times Prentice Hall, 2002)
Intellectual Capital for Communities: Nations, Regions, and Cities (Butterworth-Heinemann, 2005) (with Ahmed Bounfour)

BILL GATES
Visionary (2005 Ranking: 2)

William Henry Gates III was born in Seattle in 1955. He won a place at Harvard but dropped out, partly through lack of confidence in his teachers. In 1976 his interest in electronics propelled him to found, with his friend Paul Allen, a company for writing software for microelectronic devices called Microsoft. Their first product was a version of the programming language BASIC for the primitive Altair 8800, the first personal computer in the world.

Five years later they licensed the operating system MS DOS to IBM for use with that company's nascent personal computer. Gates and Allen retained the right to use and develop the system themselves. Gates had a mission, to put a personal computer (using Microsoft software and programming languages) on every desk and in every home. IBM felt that the PC was, at most, a fad or a toy. The personal computer market mushroomed throughout the 1980s and 1990s and with it grew the success of Microsoft.

Bill Gates likes to portray himself as something of a techno-prophet, but neither he nor Microsoft has a sure Midas touch. He was at first dismissive of the Internet, seeing it as a geek's plaything. Once he realized his mistake, he made a high-speed U-turn. The result has included Microsoft Outlook. Microsoft's operating system for networks and servers, Microsoft NT, was an expensive flop, and not a few computer professionals see Microsoft software as "bug-infested" and unreliable. Gates decided in 1998 to reorganize the company under the banner of VV2 (Vision Version 2). It was split into eight autonomous units. Gates himself, while remaining at the Microsoft helm, has taken less of a hands-on approach in recent years. He devotes more of his time to work with the Bill and Melinda Gates Foundation, the world's richest.

Bill Gates does not belong to any university faculty. He does not consult or coach. Neither does he lecture. He is not a hermit and his thoughts on management have been made widely available through his two books, *The Road Ahead* (1995) and *Business @ the Speed of Thought* (1999). His involvement with his company and with the industry as a whole has always been transparent. People could see (some of) what he was doing at Microsoft.

He has always had quite a lot to say about strategy. In the manner of management gurus, he has isolated six things that a company should do to achieve success in any market. It should:

+ Concentrate on a market with big potential and few competitors
+ Get in early and go in big
+ Set up a proprietary position
+ Protect that position using every method available
+ Aim for high gross margins or the highest available
+ Make customers an offer they find hard, if not impossible, to refuse

Microsoft is a knowledge company. Its assets are its highly skilled and creative workers. It is held together by a digital nervous system (DNS) of e-mail, allowing instant connectivity. This also allowed Gates a high degree of supervision when he was active as CEO. He could supervise and comment upon even the smallest detail of the work of individual employees.

Some visitors have likened Microsoft's headquarters to a university campus. There are lots of opportunities for brainstorming, sharing ideas, and generally interacting in as informal a way as possible.

Gates has always sought to inject the organization with vital components. There are five, all of which begin with the letter E:

+ Enrichment: employees are attracted by high salaries and retained through generous option schemes
+ Egalitarianism
+ Empowerment
+ E-mail

+ Emphasis on performance: employees' performance is assessed twice yearly; they receive a mark on a one-to-five scale. A "four" is extraordinarily good; a "one" means they are fired

Bill Gates is not a management guru in the sense of others. He does not preach, except to his own employees. He does not intimate that what works (or has worked) for Microsoft can be translated into success elsewhere. However, his very success inevitably means that what he does at Microsoft is an object of study and emulation by others.

Essential reading

http://www.microsoft.com/billgates/default.asp
The Road Ahead (Penguin, 1995)
Business @ the Speed of Thought: Using a Digital Nervous System (Warner, 1999)

MALCOLM GLADWELL
Journalist (2005 Ranking: 31)

Malcolm Gladwell was born in England in 1963 but grew up in Ontario, Canada. He attended the University of Toronto, earning a history degree in 1984. From 1987 to 1996 he worked on the staff of the *Washington Post*, first as a science writer, then as New York Bureau chief. In 1996 he joined the staff of the *New Yorker* and continues to write articles on an extensive spectrum of topics.

It is hard to categorize what Gladwell does. He has written with apparent expertise on a plethora of subjects. He may be described as an observer of social trends or as a describer of culture in the act of creation. His scope involves the worlds of science, business, and their intersections with people.

His celebrity so far rests on two books. *The Tipping Point* (2000) explores the theme that little things mean a lot. Gladwell looks for the fulcrum, that point at which loose ends become a critical mass, magically converting the ordinary into the extraordinary, the little into the many, the normal into the notable. How this happens often revolves around the character of unique human beings. Calling it "The Law of the Few," he feels that tipping points can be generated by unusual (but far from abnormal) types of people:

+ *Mavens*: these are information brokers and sources; they are people who know things, who are both teacher and student at the same time but who do not try to persuade others overtly

+ *Connectors*: these are information conduits, a kind of societal glue, who consciously disseminate ideas
+ *Salesmen*: these are sellers of ideas, people who persuade other people of the value of the information they proffer

The Law of the Few has the potential to give an idea or a product a property he calls *stickiness*. Via this occurrence, an idea or product gets attached to the general public's way of life and mode of thinking. Yet, whether it actually becomes sticky depends on many other factors – sometimes a few simple, apparently insignificant, changes or enhancements. For Gladwell, the most important tipping point factor is the right context. An often vital contextual element is the physical environment we inhabit. If it is congested, untidy, and unkempt, it can have a serious impact on our individual behavior and on the receptiveness of individuals to stimuli.

On the adoption of trends and products, he quotes from the work of Geoffrey Moore who highlights the role of different groups such as innovators, early adopters, and the early majority in the acceptance of new technology. Gladwell sees the mavens, connectors, and salesmen as having a specific role in translating the ideas of the innovators and early adopters. They adapt ideas so that they are acceptable by the majority, who are, as a rule, more risk-averse and intuitively conservative.

The Tipping Point is, as Gladwell states on his website, about *epidemics*: "As human beings, we always expect everyday change to happen slowly and steadily, and for there to be some relationship between cause and effect. And when there isn't – when crime drops dramatically in New York for no apparent reason, or when a movie made on a shoestring budget ends up making hundreds of millions of dollars – we're surprised. I'm saying, don't be surprised. This is the way social epidemics work."

In his second book, *Blink* (2005), he offers a paradox in the subtitle: how to think without thinking. He says that there are two ways to think – first, there's the spur-of-the-moment variety performed very quickly and apparently independent of the second type of thinking, careful analysis. For Gladwell, the first kind of thinking is done in a blink. This kind of thinking often evolves into split-second decision-making, but he argues that this is not to be considered random or spontaneous. Such decisions can be described as a "gut response." Yet, this doesn't mean that they are irresponsible or trivial.

The mind may well be making a perfectly sound and rational decision based on accumulated experience.

In *Blink*, Gladwell asserts that our mental faculties work so quickly that we haven't time to see what is going on. Gladwell examines the psychological phenomenon of "thin slicing," when decisions are made by zeroing in on relevant information and brushing out irrelevant noise. While snap judgment may be suspect – and analysis is considered preferable – we resort to the former only when there is an acute shortage of that luxurious but necessary commodity for analysis: *time*.

Gladwell presents examples in which snap judgments prove eventually correct; conversely, he shows how extended analysis and dissection can ultimately trigger failures. A key point for Gladwell: Humans are hopeless at analyzing their own responses. They are also less than competent at analyzing the responses of others. He suggests that many marketing errors occur because too much weight is given to data from the wrong types of test, such as blind tasting.

Both books are written in a narrative and episodic style, illustrated with quotations and examples from the real world. In November 2005 we learned that *Blink* was to become a movie. Actor-turned-producer Leonardo DiCaprio has bought the rights from Gladwell and intends to make a film tied to his concepts. Gladwell will be involved as an adviser and possible screenwriter.

Essential reading

http://www.gladwell.com/bio.html
The Tipping Point: How Little Things Can Make a Big Difference (Little, Brown, 2000)
Blink: The Power of Thinking Without Thinking (Little, Brown, 2005)

ROB GOFFEE AND GARETH JONES

Educator-Executives (2005 Ranking: 45)

Rob Goffee is Professor of Organizational Behavior at London Business School. His initial academic background was in sociology, and he earned his Ph.D. at the University of Kent at Canterbury, England.

Gareth Jones is a visiting professor at INSEAD, the international business school in Fontainebleau. He also has a background in social sciences, an interest that began at the University of East Anglia in the U.K. He then joined the Organizational Behavior Group at London Business School, becoming eventually the director of the school's Accelerated Development Programme. He left the academic world to be a manager at Polygram, returning to teaching at Henley Management College. Ultimately, he joined the British Broadcasting Corporation as director of human resources and internal communications. He is now one of Europe's most in-demand business speakers.

Goffee and Jones are the founding partners of Creative Management Associates (CMA), a consultancy focused on organizations in which creativity is a source of competitive strength.

Both men have produced much material in their own right, but it is for their collaborative work and co-authorship that they are best known. One of these, *The Character of a Corporation* (1998), continues the work done on corporate culture by Charles Handy. It contains insights derived from their work as consultants. They stress that corporate culture is not just some intangible feeling or set of emotions, but a factor of organizational health that, if not handled properly, can seriously damage profitability and effectiveness. As

Handy does, they identify four different types of organizational cultures but use their own classifications:

+ Networked
+ Mercenary
+ Fragmented
+ Communal

No one culture is good or bad, worse or better, than the others. They all have their positive and negative aspects. Take the networked culture: the good side of this is that there are good communications between people in the organization. Ideas and information flow freely and easily from where they are generated to where they are wanted and needed. However, this exemplifies a "good" network culture. "Bad" network cultures host members who gossip incessantly, spreading bogus news that may be true but which is usually detrimental to some other associate. As a result of such behavior in a bad network culture, employees soon become defensive, cliques form, and work devolves into a civil war. In time, the workplace atmosphere becomes toxic. Goffee and Jones not only analyze each of the four cultures in this way, they also give advice so readers can identify their own corporate cultures and change them for the better.

Their later work includes a 2000 *Harvard Business Review* article entitled "Why Should Anyone Be Led By You?" and a book, published in 2006, with the same title. Goffee and Jones are blunt in criticizing much current corporate leadership: too many leaders, they say, are instead bureaucrats. Happily, these two authors do not issue a clarion call for leaders to attempt to become superheroes. The good leader must try to be human, they assert; he or she should also be transparent, unafraid to show blind sides or weak spots. This is the best way to inspire others. Moreover, the inspiration transaction has to take place on the individual, one-to-one level. Organizations cannot do anything without dedicated, high-performing individuals. Good leaders recognize that everyone they lead is, at heart, an individual human being. It is thus perilous to view an array of individuals as an anonymous collective.

Good leaders have the confidence (and also the courage!) to act on intuition. This action must be informed by solid experience. Leaders must also borrow a very important asset from the acting profession's repertory of skills – good timing. An experienced actor knows the appropriateness of every action, no matter how small. Similarly, good leaders know how to manage people and events; they know how and when to be tough, but they know that toughness on its own is never a solution. They know when to temper toughness with empathy. This range of judgments and actions lies within the abilities of most people. Thus, good leaders don't have to be a Superman–Clark Kent kind of person. They just have to be uniquely and genuinely themselves.

Essential reading

http://whyshouldanyonebeledbyyou.com

The Character of a Corporation: How Your Company's Culture Can Make or Break Your Business (Harper Business, 1998)

"Why Should Anyone Be Led By You?" *Harvard Business Review*, September–October 2000, pp. 62–70

Why Should Anyone Be Led By You? (Harvard Business School Press, 2006)

DANIEL GOLEMAN
Psychologist (2005 Ranking: 42)

Daniel Goleman (born 1946) is a writer and lecturer on psychology and leadership. He was born in Stockton, California. He studied psychology at Amherst College, Massachusetts. He then embarked on postgraduate work at Harvard, earning a masters degree and a doctorate in clinical psychology. He later taught on the Harvard faculty. For many years he was a regular contributor to the *New York Times* on psychology and mental health issues.

In the early 1990s he began research into problems that were affecting American schools at the time. These included student aggression, depression, and the lack of empathy among students for co-learners and teachers. He worked out a theory of emotional intelligence, based on extensive research. The results were published in *Emotional Intelligence* (1995). Emotional intelligence was separate from and, in Goleman's view, superior to traditional rational intelligence, the type measured in IQ tests. "We can be effective only when the two systems – the emotional brain and the thinking brain – work together." The cornerstone of emotional intelligence is the ability to control and use emotions effectively. The term, although now irrevocably linked with Goleman, was not his initially, having been coined first by the Israeli psychologist Reuven Bar-On.

In his next book, *Working with Emotional Intelligence* (1998), Goleman sought to expand on emotional intelligence in action and how it could enhance personal and professional effectiveness. It was a necessary skill for anyone working within an organization and alongside others on a daily basis. The existence of emotional issues within the workplace had been ignored. Emotions of any sort were considered superfluous in the business world or the workplace. Goleman stated that emotions were needed by all, but especially by leaders. Those holding senior executive positions were usually well endowed with traditional rational intelligence or IQ. What could make them stand apart from other managers was utilization of emotional intelligence. Goleman felt that this could be achieved fairly easily, as emotional intelligence could be acquired, maybe after some application. It involved developing five skills or personality attributes:

+ Self-awareness
+ Managing emotions
+ Motivating others
+ Showing empathy
+ Staying connected

In *The New Leaders* (2002) and *Primal Leadership* (2002), Goleman and a team of collaborators carried out extensive research on 3,000 executives in American corporations. There had been a lot of talk about leadership styles but not much hard data. His findings were that the signals and messages emanating from leadership figures had a decisive bearing on how employees throughout the organization viewed management and the overall attributes of the workplace. Goleman stressed the need for leaders to create a "resonant" leadership. He also identified six different styles of leadership closely tied to emotional intelligence. These were:

+ Coercive leadership: demanding immediate and unquestioning compliance
+ Authoritative leadership: mobilizing towards a shared vision
+ Affiliative leadership: creating emotional bonds and harmony
+ Democratic leadership: building consensus through participation
+ Pacesetting leadership: expecting self-direction
+ Coaching leadership: developing people for the future

None of these was any better or worse than the others. In fact, rather than an individual displaying one particular leadership trait, as had been common in the past, Goleman argued that the successful leader would have to be able to deploy a suite of these leadership styles in different situations. Human emotions are not easily pigeonholed, so the model is far from set in cement.

Goleman's work has proved very influential. *Emotional Intelligence* has been translated into 33 languages; *Working with Emotional Intelligence* into 26. Many organizations such as American Express have started to pay more attention to emotional competence issues. The U.S. Army found it was able to save nearly $3 million in training costs through an emotional intelligence initiative.

Essential reading

http://www.eiconsortium.org/members/goleman.htm
Emotional Intelligence: Why It Can Matter More Than IQ (Bantam, 1995)
Working with Emotional Intelligence (Bantam, 1998)
The New Leaders: Transforming the Art of Leadership into the Science of Results (Time Warner, 2002) (with Richard Boyatzis and Annie McKee)
Primal Leadership: Realizing the Power of Emotional Intelligence (Harvard Business School Press, 2002) (with Richard Boyatzis and Annie McKee)

VIJAY GOVINDARAJAN
Educator (2005 Ranking: 30)

Vijay Govindarajan (or VG as everyone calls him both from affection and for convenience) is the Earl C. Daum 1924 Professor of International Business at the Tuck School of Business of Dartmouth College in Hanover, New Hampshire. He is also founder-director of Tuck's Center for Global Learning.

He acknowledges the unique influence of his grandfather on his life. His grandfather used to gather together informal groups of people – adults and children – under the spreading boughs of a banyan tree in his home village in southern India. There they would discuss issues of common interest. He helped all, including young children having difficulty with their homework.

VG trained as an accountant in India, earning the Presidential Gold Medal for coming first out of 10,000 candidates in the Indian CPA's final exams. He then left India to pursue further study at Harvard and Michigan State University. After earning his Ph.D., he taught in India and the U.S. before finally joining the Tuck faculty in 1985. He has also been a visiting professor at Harvard Business School and the International University of Japan.

Apart from his teaching commitments, he works widely as a consultant. He has not yet established a separate organization to promote the VG "brand."

VG has contributed greatly to thinking about business strategy. He has developed his "Box 1-2-3 strategy" for any organization attempting to pursue new initiatives. The first box is the present that has to be managed. Many organizations think this is all there is to strategy. It is important, but it is not the only set of issues. More vital are the other two boxes: the past, which has to

- An eventual creation and pooling of collective viewpoints
+ Humans have souls. This means they
  - Have a sense of identity
  - Can get inspired and feel passionate about things, including their work
  - Can join the team or stand on the sidelines

Gratton believes that successful companies should have souls as well. They must monitor and improve their organization's emotional health. The two central points to a corporate soul are commitment and trust. Employees must be encouraged to build deeper trust and exercise greater commitment: neither can be commanded out of thin air. They can be nurtured only in an environment of reciprocity.

The book gives practical advice about making reality out of theory. It does this through a series of steps to be adopted to implement the living strategy. There are also references to companies like HP and GlaxoSmithKline that are pursuing living strategies.

In *The Democratic Enterprise* (2004), Gratton describes how to build a company based on choice and commitment, where people want to work because it gives them more than just a paycheck. Creating such a business is not easy. The starting point is recognizing that the individuals are bigger than their assigned roles.

There are four essential ingredients to the recipe:

+ Creation and support for individual autonomy
+ Creation of organizational insight
+ Construction of organizational variety
+ Construction and crafting of a sense of shared destiny

The result should be a mixed dish – offering speed, flexibility, and commitment. It should be a company in which:

+ Talented employees can breathe and develop
+ Employees are understood as well as customers

- Work content is designed in a flexible way, giving people choice
- There is shared meaning and purpose

Too many employers in the past have treated their employees like children; the latter have, not surprisingly, responded accordingly. Companies should allow employees more choice about how, where, and even when they work. This leads to greater commitment. Gratton offers eight in-depth examples of enterprises where this is happening:

- *Astra Zeneca*: transparency in employee access to information about pay and benefits
- *British Petroleum*: internal markets for jobs
- *British Telecom*: greater locational choice for employees
- *Goldman Sachs*: choice around development of relationships
- *Hewlett-Packard*: discretion around time issues
- *McKinsey & Co.*: great transparency in choice of projects by associates
- *Sony*: engineers have freedom to create meaningful jobs
- *Unisys*: access to enhanced training opportunities for employees

Essential reading

http://www.lyndagratton.com/
Strategic Human Resource Management: Corporate Rhetoric and Human Reality (Oxford University Press, 1999)
Living Strategy: Putting People at the Heart of Corporate Purpose (Financial Times Prentice Hall, 2000)
The Democratic Enterprise: Liberating your Business with Freedom, Flexibility and Commitment (Financial Times Prentice Hall, 2004)

ALAN GREENSPAN
Economist (2005 Ranking: 35)

Alan Greenspan (born 1926) was chairman of the U.S. Federal Reserve Board from 1987 until 2005.

He was born in New York City. He studied economics at New York University, gaining a Ph.D. He worked for over three decades with Townsend-Greenspan & Company, an economics consultancy firm in New York. He also gained experience working for the public sector as the chairman of President Gerald Ford's Council of Economic Advisers, and in the early 1980s as Chairman of the National Commission on Social Security Reform. He has also been an economic adviser to a number of public and private bodies, including the editorial board of *Time* magazine.

He received a true baptism of fire in his new role at the Fed: the serious and abrupt disruption in the Wall Street equities market occurred a little over a month after his appointment. Although this could have been as serious as the infamous crash of 1929, one of the reasons it was not is generally considered to be the action of the Federal Reserve in pumping liquidity into the market. The U.S. economy stumbled, but it did not fall. In the next decade it experienced unrivalled years of successive growth. Much of this was due to Greenspan's "steady-as-she-goes" stewardship. He stood in the center of economic debate, aiming to avoid inflationary pressures, but at the same time not being a hostage to fundamentalist anti-inflationism. Once he had set his course, no bluster from businessmen or politicians distracted him.

There were voices raised against his perceived monetary conservatism, especially when the U.S. economy was riding high on the wave of "technophoria" in the mid and late 1990s. The economy should not be provoked into overheating, he felt, as it was already demonstrating signs of "irrational exuberance." His talismanic position was manifestly demonstrated by his utterance of those two words in 1996. Some markets dropped as much as five percent in value. The Dow went down by two percentage points. It is fruitless to calculate how much equity value was wiped out by those two words. It took Genghis Khan far longer to wreak equivalent havoc. But Greenspan was only speaking candidly about stock prices that seemed to be entering a stratosphere of unreality.

It is an open secret that he was not too uncomfortable at leaving his position and that he wanted to leave earlier. He has found it difficult to deal with some of the Bush administration's domestic economic policies, as well as its often-defensive postures on world trade issues.

Greenspan has not had time to write down his thoughts on economics, or on anything else. Upon his retirement in January 2006, he will have a little more time on his hands, so some works from his fingers can be expected. Numerous books have been written about him though. He knows the impact that his utterances, whether in print or speech, have on U.S. and world markets. He is aware that, like anyone associated with a powerful institution, it is not so much what he says as what he does not say. Every statement, no matter how banal or unrelated, is devoured and analyzed by economists, stock analysts, journalists, business pundits, and politicians. The same process is often applied to what lies between the lines.

Behind the economist playing dice with the world economy, if not with the universe, appears to be a man of great integrity. He has said: "I have found no greater satisfaction than achieving success through honest dealing and strict adherence to the view that, for you to gain, those you deal with should gain as well."

Essential reading

http://www.federalreserve.gov/bios/greenspan.htm
David B. Sicilia, *Greenspan Effect: Words That Move the World's Markets* (McGraw-Hill, 1999)

ANDREW GROVE
Executive (2005 Ranking: 41)

Andy Grove is now senior adviser to executive management at Intel Corporation, having previously been chairman, CEO, and president. He has also taught part-time at Stanford's business school.

Andy Grove was born in Budapest, Hungary, in 1936. He lost half his hearing when he was four and also contracted scarlet fever, which left him with a weak heart. He emigrated to America in the wake of the crushing of the Hungarian Revolution by Soviet tanks in 1956. He studied chemical engineering at City College, New York, and gained a Ph.D. from U.C.-Berkeley. He joined the research laboratory of a small computer company, Fairchild Semiconductor, established by Geoffrey Moore and Robert Noyce, later the founders of Intel. When they set up the latter company in 1968, Grove joined them as employee number four. He became president of the company in 1979 and CEO in 1987. He is the author of five books and a large number of articles and papers, covering a wide spectrum from computer science to business and motivation.

At Intel he oversaw the move away from semiconductor memory towards a microprocessor on a single chip. This culminated in the development in 1971 of the Intel 4004. More chip-based microprocessors followed. Grove battled hard against competition from firms like Motorola to have Intel's 8088 microprocessor adopted by IBM for its personal computers (PCs). During his watch as CEO, Grove gained the gratitude of investors when Intel's stock price went up 24 times.

He holds several patents on semiconductor and computer technology applications.

Grove has noted the many lessons he has learned as a manager and CEO in a number of best-selling books. In *High-Output Management* (1983), he outlined some of his core principles of management, such as:

+ Convert subordinates and co-workers into highly productive team members
+ Motivate these teams to attain peak performance
+ Combine conceptual elegance with a practical understanding of the real-life scenarios that managers encounter every day

In the book, these principles were accompanied by practical advice about production, inspection, and the use of targets.

The defensively titled *Only the Paranoid Survive* (1996) has been even more successful. This is a warts-and-all appraisal of the highs and lows of Intel, its successes, its failures, and how the company and its boss have learned from them. He defends his reference to paranoia early on: "… [W]hen it comes to business I believe in the value of paranoia. Business success contains the seeds of its own destruction. The more successful you are, the more people want a chunk of your business, and then another and then another until there is nothing left."

Grove sees management as being unpredictable. It is punctuated by what he terms strategic inflection points (SIPs), times when all the rules and paradigms of business go up in the air and the earth starts trembling. These require fundamental changes in strategy, technology, and organization. SIPs can be caused by the technological developments of competitors or changes in regulations. Sometimes they seem insignificant at first and only reveal their true nature later. The good manager has to be able to recognize them when they happen; better still to anticipate them. One SIP outlined in detail by Grove was the chaos that ensued after a minor technical fault was found in its Pentium processor in late 1994. Another situation occurred when Intel became aware that Japanese manufacturers were able to make better and cheaper memory chips than Intel. Grove responded, but it took Intel three years and a lot of money to regain its competitive advantage.

Despite his advocacy of management paranoia, Grove takes an optimistic approach to technology: "A fundamental rule in technology says that whatever *can* be done *will* be done."

His book *Swimming Across: A Memoir* (2001) tells of his experiences growing up in Hungary during World War II when many of his relatives were sent to Auschwitz and of the poverty and hardships of the post-war years. This was a side of his life which he had avoided talking about until comparatively recently.

Essential reading

http://www.intel.com/pressroom/kits/bios/grove.htm
High-Output Management (Random House, 1983)
One on One With Andy Grove: How to Manage Your Boss, Yourself and Your Co-Workers (Putnam, 1987)
Only the Paranoid Survive (Currency, 1996)
Swimming Across: A Memoir (Warner, 2001)

GARY HAMEL
Consultant (2005 Ranking: 14)

Gary Hamel (born 1954) is founder and chief executive officer of Strategos, a consultancy based in Palo Alto, California. He earned his Ph.D. at the University of Michigan, Ann Arbor, in international business. That was where he met and got to know C. K. Prahalad. While the latter stayed on in Ann Arbor, Hamel crossed the Atlantic and spent a year teaching the M.B.A. course at the London Business School. He liked teaching but was afraid of becoming a Monday morning quarterback of the management world. He yearned to roll up his sleeves and get involved in the real business world. He felt a near-evangelical destiny to help companies – and so help everyone else. He left academia, establishing Strategos in 1993.

Hamel's contributions to management thinking are found in the well-attended lectures he gives around the world each year, as well as in his publications. These include numerous articles, some of which have won awards, and books such as *Competing for the Future* (1995) (written with C. K. Prahalad), and *Leading the Revolution* (2002). His style is deliberately anecdotal, illustrating points with clear examples.

Central to his thinking are the concepts of industry foresight, strategic intent, and the recognition of core competencies. Many companies are locked in the past. They may be employing out-of-date technologies and work practices. These kinds of companies are big on command-and-control, but they stifle innovative thinking. They may be pursuing growth and competitiveness by a constant, and maybe doomed, process of downsizing accompanied by slashing costs left, right, and center. They may also be locked in competitive strategies that pit them against industry rivals. According to Hamel, the past must be forgotten in favor of the future and a *strategic intent.*

Strategic intent is bigger and broader than just strategy. He gives an example: John F. Kennedy's commitment to put an American on the moon before the end of the 1960s. It was bold, many felt that it was foolish and unattainable, but Kennedy's advisers knew it was doable. A lot of hurdles had to be cleared, but the intention became a goal, a Holy Grail, that focused minds. A strategic intent may seem like folly, but it is achievable. That places it on a different plane from daydreams or corporate fantasy.

A company can determine what is fantasy and what is realizable by referring to their core competencies. These can be discovered by asking the following questions:

+ What makes us unique?
+ How do we satisfy our customers?
+ How can we find new ways of doing this?

As an example of a company that has done this successfully, Hamel cites book retailer Barnes & Noble. The appearance of Jeff Bezos' Amazon.com seemed to sound B&N's death knell by offering far lower prices and a different buying experience. Amazon did not worry about a network of bricks-and-mortar stores and staff. Barnes & Noble realized that its bookstores were not liabilities but were among its core competencies. It fitted them out with places to sit and relax, coffee bars, and areas where kids could play with toys. B&N offered a new – and different – buying experience.

Hamel says he writes for everyone in an organization, be they "the big cheese" at the top, or the frustrated inhabitants of a "rat cubicle." Companies must identify the revolutionaries in their ranks who may well be sulking in the cubicles. Instead of shooting revolutionaries, as in the past, they should harness their ideas and energies. Hamel's *agents provocateurs* (wherever they be) are usually motivated by ten "precepts" (he doesn't call them commandments). They must have:

+ Unrealistic expectations
+ Elastic business goals and definitions

 + A cause that inspires them
 + An ear for advice and experience
 + An open market for ideas
 + An open market for capital so investors can fund experimentation
 + An open market for talent
 + A positive, encouraging attitude to low-risk experimentation
 + A cellular organization
 + A positive attitude to personal wealth accumulation

Hamel likes revolutionaries and he does not discriminate in favor of dress codes, age, or appearance. Revolutionaries may even have gray hair – or maybe none at all. These people work for and run companies that continually redefine and reinvent themselves and so maintain their value to customers. An example of a "gray revolutionary" for Hamel is online stockbroker Charles Schwab.

Essential reading

http://www.garyhamel.com/
Competing for the Future (Harvard Business School Press, 1995) (with C. K. Prahalad)
Leading the Revolution (Harvard Business School Press, 2002)

CHARLES HANDY
Social Philosopher (2005 Ranking: 10)

Charles Handy (born 1932) is Irish by birth. He was brought up in the genteel poverty of an Anglican parsonage in a still-rural part of County Kildare. He pursued his education at Oriel College, Oxford, and then joined Royal Dutch Shell. The prospect of a posting to Liberia caused Handy to leave Shell in favor of a position as professor of business management in the newly founded London Business School. In the mid '70s he worked for an expert group based at Windsor Castle, before deciding to plow his own furrow in life as a writer, lecturer, and consultant.

Handy coined the term "portfolio worker" for someone who worked independently of an organization and whose living was drawn from a number of differing elements, as in a share portfolio. Many people faced this future. The growth of small, individually run firms, especially in the U.K., has borne him out.

His first book, *Inside Organizations* (1976), was an account of contemporary business structure. Some critics said that he had only put forward old and accepted ideas in a new way.

It was only when Handy parachuted out of the world of secure employment that his talents as a writer on management (and much else) blossomed. In *The Age of Unreason* (1989) he proposed the Shamrock organization as a business model. Many have tied the symbol to his Irish background. The shamrock has long been powerful in the Anglican Church of Ireland because of its apocryphal use by St. Patrick as a symbol of the Holy Trinity. For Handy, the first of the three leaves represented the professional managers and administrators – the organizational core. This leaf is shrinking in size. The second leaf contained the contractual fringe. Its contributors to the organization were vital, but they were outsiders. In the third leaf were portfolio workers as well as temporary workers and part-timers. They contributed much, but they could never be considered part of the organization. Many didn't want to be; they wanted jobs but not careers. They frequently worked for a number of disparate organizations. In Handy's language they were like fleas feeding off elephants. The latter were the large organizations, the mega-corporations, an analogy he pursued in the autobiographical *The Elephant and the Flea* (2001).

When he writes about management Handy is never prescriptive. He thinks it is a fallacy to believe that there is one, correct style of management. In *Gods of Management* (1995) he isolates four different management styles or cultures and draws an analogy between these and religious cults in ancient Greece. The partisans of Zeus he compares to those belonging to a club-like organization. The partisans of Apollo follow a rank culture, found in bureaucracies and large organizations. Followers of Athena believe in a task-based culture, often working in teams, while the Dionysians are bigger than any organization to which they might belong. They are typified by profession-als like lawyers. No culture is better than the others. Some are simply better suited to certain contexts. Any of the four could achieve results, but they should never be forced on an organization that has a different culture.

Reading Charles Handy is like having a conversation in a leafy vicarage on a Sunday afternoon. Handy directs the discussion but not in a domineering way. His contributions are peppered with opinionated and frequently amus-ing asides. His comments are made in a deferentially certain manner.

Handy does not see himself as a management guru, but as a social philoso-pher. He laments that blind greed still motivates too many: "We have created a mercenary society. Getting richer and richer, and bigger and bigger, has become a substitute for not believing in what we are doing."

Handy's writings and activities are far-flung. He has always had much to say (frequently critical) about education. His own education did not prepare him for "life as a flea." He believes that little has changed since. Many people face a flea existence, but they have been given neither the emotional nor the intellectual tools for it. People will have to craft their own futures, he says, and he helps those who try. Handy was involved in the development of the

Open University's M.B.A. program, insisting on the incorporation of practical, "on-the-job" elements.

He is a frequent broadcaster; this includes his accessible series for the BBC World Service, *The Handy Guide to the Gurus of Management*.

Essential reading

http://www.forumforcorporateconscience.com/agenda/handy.html
The Age of Unreason (Harvard Business School Press, 1989)
Gods of Management (Oxford University Press, 1995)
The Elephant and the Flea: Looking Backwards to the Future (Harvard Business School Press, 2001)

GEERT HOFSTEDE
Researcher (2005 Ranking: 47)

Geert Hofstede (born 1928) is a Senior Fellow of the Institute for Research on Intercultural Cooperation (IRIC), and Extra-Mural Fellow of the Center for Economic Research at Tilburg University in the Netherlands. He was formerly Professor of Organizational Anthropology and International Management at Maastricht University.

He holds a masters degree in mechanical engineering from Delft University and a Ph.D. in social science from the University of Groningen. In a wide-ranging life, he has worked in many different fields apart from the academic. He was a ship's engineer in the 1940s. He also worked in an Amsterdam factory. He was a senior psychologist with IBM, which provided him with a rich reservoir of data. The result was *Culture's Consequences* (1981), based on over 10,000 questionnaires sent to IBM staff members in over 60 countries.

Cultural studies have been around for a long time, but nobody had bothered to apply them to the world of management. Multinationals headquartered in one country, but with subsidiaries in many others, were a perfect environment for examining cultural assertions and conflicts.

For Hofstede a culture is "the collective programming of the mind which distinguishes the members of one group or category of people from another." Each culture has its own symbols, heroes, values, rituals, and practices. He distinguished four (later raised to five) national cultural categories based on responses to authority, time, and space. These were:

+ Power distance: "the extent to which the less powerful members of organizations ... accept and expect that power is distributed unequally"

+ Individualism/collectivism: the degree to which "the ties that bind" are loose or all-embracing
+ Masculinity/femininity: the distribution of roles between genders, as well as differences in attitudes between assertiveness (masculinity) and sensitivity and empathy (femininity)
+ Uncertainty avoidance: coping with ambiguity – uncertainty-averse cultures avoid ambiguity by rules and unquestioning belief in absolute truth; they may also be intolerant of dissent
+ Long/short-term orientation: long-termers value perseverance and truth; they put a lot of store in tradition, fulfilling social obligations and saving face, especially in Eastern cultures

Hofstede found that countries with a "Latin" culture – Spain, Italy, and Latin America – had high acceptance of power distance. They were also uncertainty averse. He put this down to values inherited from the Roman Empire, political centralization, and an all-pervasive legal system.

Individualism was strong in the developed world; collectivism strong in developing countries; masculinity was high in Japan and Germanic countries; femininity high in Nordic nations and the Netherlands. Uncertainty aversion was high in Japan and German-speaking cultures, but low in English-speaking, Nordic, and Chinese countries. Long-term orientations were common in East Asian countries.

Hofstede distinguishes between national and organizational cultures and says the two are separate. National cultures are based on values, organizational cultures on practices. National and linguistic boundaries have no effect. Different organizational cultures are found in one country. The five-part model for national culture is inapplicable to organizations. For organizations, Hofstede drew up instead a six-point framework based on:

+ Process versus results orientation
+ Job versus employee orientation
+ Professional versus parochial worldview
+ Open versus closed systems
+ Tightly versus loosely controlled organizations and practices
+ Pragmatic versus normative practices

Organizational culture is vital in business: it is what holds an organization together, especially when it operates in disparate markets. Where an organization stands is often determined by what industry it is in. Cross-cultural management is based on handling both national and organizational cultures at the same time. The latter can be modified over time; changing national cultural dimensions is a far riskier and more difficult project. It is probably best to accept the given dimensions and deal with their positive aspects.

The need for cross-cultural management, whether of organizations, markets, or brands, has been made much more acute by globalization. The spread of the English language may appear to be homogenizing the world, but this is a delusion. National cultural differences are still deeply entrenched and are ignored at an organization's peril.

Essential reading

http://www.geert-hofstede.com

Culture's Consequences: International Differences in Work-related Values (McGraw-Hill, 1981)

Cultures and Organizations: Software of the Mind (Intercultural Press, 1994)

Exploring Culture: Exercises, Stories and Synthetic Cultures (Intercultural Press, 2002)

ROSABETH MOSS KANTER

Educator (2005 Ranking: 19)

Rosabeth Moss Kanter (born 1943) is the Ernest Arbuckle Professor of Business Administration at Harvard Business School.

Her background is in sociology. She was a fellow of the Harvard Law School before gaining a tenured professorship in business at Yale. In 1986 she returned to Harvard's Business School. She is the author of numerous books and articles and also has her own consultancy and research company, Goodmeasure, based in Boston. She says that consulting helps to keep her creative and allows her to apply what she learns to real-life situations. She is also a frequent guest lecturer and speaker.

Men and Women of the Corporation (1977) examined, among other things, how the corporate workplace was dominated by male-held stereotypes. Women were still an exotic species in middle and top management. Their rarity made them targets of male prejudice and ignorance.

In the 1980s, her interests broadened to include the phenomenon of change in organizations and its impact on members and the communities where they operated. Corporate America was entering a period of profound transformation to the post-entrepreneurial society. To survive, organizations would have to change their structures and behavior. What they had to do was outlined in books like *The Change Masters* (1988) and the quirkily titled *When Giants Learn to Dance* (1989). Hierarchies would be replaced by smaller, flatter organizations. They would be flexible, fast, focused, friendly, and most importantly – *fun*. The new corporate environment would be dominated by "PAL" partnerships resulting from pooling, allying, and linking. The successful managers would be business athletes. They would carry their ideas by their arguments and personalities. They would co-operate with colleagues. They would be all-round players – superb strikers but also good in defense and midfield. They would possess a portfolio of talents that could be plugged in anywhere. Their reputation would be beyond reproach. Like the best superstars, they would be quite humble, even cuddly.

Kanter has continued her researches by looking at how the Internet has affected companies. In *E.volve!* (2001) she used her sociological training to carry out in-depth, questionnaire-based research with hundreds of firms throughout the world. These were condensed into case studies (not a surprising format, perhaps, given where she works). She examined how the business world was evolving in the information age. She also has seven prescriptions for today's business leaders. They must:

+ Lead by ideas
+ Be good at communications (receiving as well as giving, both a good communicator and a good listener)
+ Be cosmopolitan, not imprisoned by stereotypes
+ Be good with complexity
+ Be curious
+ Care about their customers and workers
+ View employees as resources, not subordinates

There is as great a need as ever for strategy according to Kanter; however, the strategy that will work best is not that of a Clausewitz or a Napoleon. It is more at home in the theater than on the battlefield. The new strategist should be like the director of a play. A co-operative spirit that values teamwork over hierarchy is the best, maybe the only approach.

Kanter is also interested in the impact of the Internet and global connectivity on wider society. Although she is never shy about prophesying, she admits that her prognostications may be no more than wishful thinking. The Internet has a potential for great good and universal harm. It can be good not only for business but also for communities, breaking down barriers of distance and distrust. It can have the opposite effect, causing isolation and dependence on personal computers. Reality can become a virtual world peopled with virtual personalities, none of whom would have any responsibilities. The potential for both outcomes exists. It is up to humans to decide which one they want.

Her latest book, *Confidence* (2004), is based once again on extensive research. Confidence is central to success in many areas, not just business. It can flow in vicious cycles, sometimes spiraling downwards. It can be harnessed for greater effect through virtuous cycles. Confidence is an essential part of leadership. Leaders create confidence by setting high (though attainable) standards. They should then embody those standards and put processes in place to attain success.

Essential reading

http://www.goodmeasure.com/

Men and Women of the Corporation (Basic Books, 1977)

The Change Masters: Innovation and Entrepreneurship in the American Corporation (Simon and Schuster, 1983)

When Giants Learn to Dance: Managing the Challenges of Strategy, Management and Careers in the 1990s (Simon and Schuster, 1989)

E.volve! Succeeding in the Digital Culture of Tomorrow (Harvard Business School Press, 2001)

Confidence: How Winning Streaks and Losing Streaks Begin and End (Crown, 2004)

ROBERT KAPLAN AND DAVID NORTON
Educators (2005 Ranking: 22)

Robert S. Kaplan is the Marvin Bower Professor of Leadership Development at Harvard Business School. His background is in electrical engineering. He received bachelors and masters degrees from the Massachusetts Institute of Technology, and a doctorate in organizational research from Cornell. He taught for 16 years at Carnegie-Mellon's Graduate School of Industrial Administration (GSIA), before joining the faculty of Harvard Business School in 1984.

Much of Robert Kaplan's work has been dedicated to the topic of isolating and redefining costs. In *Relevance Lost: The Rise and Fall of Management Accounting* (1987), he lamented the decline of management accounting, which had been superseded by financial reporting. Important costs were going unrecognized, and this was having a serious impact on companies' profitability. Throughout the 1980s he pioneered the concept of activity-based costing (ABC), which looks particularly at the place of overhead and indirect costs to a business. These had often been misapplied in traditional accounting, leading to a skewed interpretation of a company's financial health. ABC was not intended to be simple. It involves taking a whole new approach to activities and the constituents that comprise them. Many companies have drawn back from fully implementing it, preferring to stay with their old tried-and-tested methods. However, Kaplan has earned considerably from consulting to those firms that have been prepared to embrace ABC. Other support services, including software providers, have stepped in with products. Among the firms that implemented ABC was Chrysler (before its marriage to Daimler). It discovered that the cost of some important components was a whopping 30 times higher than had previously been calculated and costed. This led to greater reliance on outsourcing of production.

In the late 1980s and early 1990s there was growing unease about financial reporting at the corporate board level, especially in public companies. Many felt that it was being driven by the short-term demands of the stock market and institutional investors. Kaplan, along with David Norton, president of consulting company Renaissance Strategy Group, wrote a paper for the *Harvard Business Review* in early 1992 titled "The Balanced Scorecard: Measures That Drive Results." It argued for a much broader approach to accounting and measurement, beyond the purely financial. Other perspectives should be included, such as:

+ Market/Customer perspective: "Identifying the value propositions that will be delivered to individual segments becomes the key for developing measures and objectives ..."
+ Internal perspectives: what the company should be doing internally to create added value for customers and shareholders
+ Innovation and organizational learning: how the company can create value in the future and the elements it should measure to ensure this
+ Employee perspective: turnover and the percentage of employees in direct contact with customers

It is important to invest for the future and not just in traditional investment areas; however, financial concerns should not be jettisoned. Standard financial measures can provide key linkages across the other balanced scorecard perspectives.

Kaplan and Norton believe the balanced scorecard approach would help companies identify what they must do to remain important players in the future. It will help companies turn strategy into targets and show them how goals can be achieved. The balanced scorecard has the ability to act as a unifying structure for elements within company activity that would otherwise remain diffuse, like product redesign and customer management. It also gives a more unified picture of the company as a whole, rather than as an aggregate of different, maybe competing, parts. At the same time it produces goals and targets that are of use to local managers. Kaplan and Norton's work was welcomed by many in organizations, particularly some branches of marketing and human resource management. Those branches considered it a vindication of what they had been saying for years, only to be shouted down by people in the finance department.

Kaplan and Norton came together again to produce a survey of the balanced scorecard in action in *The Strategy-Focused Organization* (2000).

Essential reading

http://www.bscol.com/bscol/leadership/

The Balanced Scorecard: Translating Strategy into Action (Harvard Business School Press, 1996) (Kaplan and Norton)

Cost and Effect (Harvard Business School Press, 1997) (Kaplan)

The Strategy-Focused Organization: How Balanced Scorecard Companies Thrive in the New Business Environment (Harvard Business School Press, 2000) (Kaplan and Norton)

MANFRED KETS DE VRIES

Educator (2005 Ranking: 32)

Manfred Kets de Vries holds the Raoul de Vitry d'Avaucourt Chair of Human Resources Management at INSEAD, Fontainebleau, France. He studied economics at Amsterdam University and then received an M.B.A. and D.B.A. from Harvard. He subsequently studied psychoanalysis at the Canadian Psychoanalytic Institute for seven years. He has taught at McGill University, L'Ecole des Hautes Etudes Commerciales de Montreal, and Harvard Business School. He is the author of over 20 books and consults widely.

Kets de Vries has put the topic of management on to the analyst's couch, as can be seen in his study of the 1990s' fad of "downsizing." His research found that this does not lead to increased efficiency. It leads to an attitude akin to bereavement following a catastrophe or a massacre. Those who were left suffered from "survivor syndrome": they felt guilty. They asked themselves why they had been spared. Top managers felt like executioners. Kets De Vries put this down to the wrong packaging of downsizing. It should have been presented as part of a firm's transformation and long-term objectives, not just short-term cost reduction.

He has also studied leadership and organization behavior. His research has included the darker underside of organizations and examinations of executives who promise much but seriously malfunction. He explored this in works like *Prisoners of Leadership* (1990) and *Leaders, Fools and Imposters* (1993).

Many CEOs are obsessive. Business is the sole motivator in their lives, and other parts of life, like personal relationships, are neglected. The real disease suffered by too many CEOs is the neurosis of narcissism. Not all narcissism is bad; a certain amount of self-love and self-belief is not only benign but also necessary in a management figure. Kets de Vries calls this constructive narcissism. Like many psychoanalysts, he traces it back to childhood. Constructive narcissism is nurtured by a settled, supportive domestic environment. The other is malign narcissism, which he calls reactive narcissism. Much of this can be traced back to a childhood that was anything but stable and happy. This may have positive outcomes if the person decides that they want to make things good for people, precisely because they had such a rough time when young. All too often it leads to the Monte Cristo syndrome – (also known as the Kenny Rogers syndrome – you're not really cheatin', you're just gettin' even). You have goals but you will use anyone and any method to attain them. This type of CEO loses all sense of boundaries to reality. He does not like hearing bad news or criticism, so he only gets filtered information and lots of praise.

Kets de Vries has also written about leadership charisma. He believes it is an illusion, that people project their fantasies on to a leadership figure. The charismatic leader can usually get results if he tries. He must inspire, perhaps through rhetorical gifts. He should be a good communicator using symbols that ring the right notes. The charismatic leader should have a good memory and be able to recall people's names unaided. He should also have the Teddy Bear factor – the ability to make people feel comfortable around him. However, one can be a very effective leader without charisma.

One of the assets of an effective leader is to know his weaknesses and to be able to effectively delegate. Kets de Vries calls this the creation of an executive role constellation.

He believes that there is still a need for the heroic leader, the one who battles against the odds and turns around a flagging business. This is true in spite of an apparent shift away from the macho to the quiet leader type. In a world beset by change and uncertainty, many feel insecure. They look for and follow a strong leader because he seems to offer them protection. This is true of all cultures, not just the more individualistic cultures of the West. He is dismissive of the often-destructive role of the media in leadership creation. He commented, "[T]he moment you get on the front of *Fortune* or *Business-Week,* it's the beginning of the end."

Essential reading

http://www.insead.edu/facultyresearch/faculty/profiles/mketsdevries/

The Neurotic Organization (Jossey-Bass, 1983) (with D. Miller)

The Happiness Equation: A Winning Formula for Happiness and Success (Vermilion, 2002) (with Elisabet Engellau)

Are Leaders Born or Are They Made? The Case of Alexander the Great (Karnac, 2004) (with Elisabet Engellau)

RAKESH KHURANA
Educator (2005 Ranking: 33)

....

Rakesh Khurana (born 1967) is associate professor of organizational behavior at Harvard Business School. He earned a bachelor's degree from Cornell University. After founding Cambridge Technology Partners, he returned to graduate study, earning a masters degree in sociology and a Ph.D. in organization behavior, both from Harvard. After teaching at MIT for two years he moved back to Harvard.

Professor Khurana has applied much of the work of sociologist Max Weber, especially social network theory, to the world of top-level management.

His greatest contribution to management studies to date has been a study of the CEO jobs market, published as *Searching for a Corporate Savior* (2002). Khurana considers that its restrictions and secretive nature mean that it cannot be considered a proper market at all.

It's tough at the top, according to Khurana. Leadership has its privileges, but complacency is rewarded by a parting of the ways. It has been estimated that two-thirds of the world's leading companies have changed their chief executive officers since 1995. Leadership expert Warren Bennis has applied a unique moniker to the phenomenon – CEO churn. Rakesh Khurana, while still at MIT, found that CEOs appointed after 1985 were three times more likely to be fired than those appointed earlier. He asked what was causing this volatility.

According to Khurana, the answer can be found in the business world. Until the last 20 years, CEOs usually emerged from the ranks of organizations where they had spent their working lives. The growth of investor capitalism has spelled a shift in corporate politics in publicly quoted companies. Large institutional investors interested in good returns on investment and high multiples are not content to remain passive in companies where they have large chunks of equity. In the past two decades, many have lost confidence in CEOs. They no longer trust that CEOs have their interests at heart. When a company fails to deliver, the institutional investors have used their muscle to engineer a change. The chief is dropped in favor of someone who promises better performance. This corporate savior (as Khurana calls him) is nearly always found outside the company. He may know nothing about the company or even the industry. He may lack managerial or strategic skills, but he has charisma, combined with a reputation as a new economy guy prepared to let talent in the organization take risks.

A rarified niche labor market has opened up for superstar CEOs who tend to have the same multicultural backgrounds. Their track records have usually included a few high-profile corporate turnarounds. Increasingly they are difficult to distinguish from one another. The corporate savior must have widespread credibility – street cred – Wall Street cred. The methods for choosing a savior are attended with much secrecy and nobody really knows what goes on, not even highly placed company insiders. That the selection of such powerful people is still clouded in obfuscation is not good for the image of corporate America.

Once chosen, the CEO brings his kudos and charisma with him. The investment community, whether stock analysts or investors, expects great things, and so the stock price rises – to the delight of the big institutional investors. There is often a simplistic inflating of the role of the CEO in a company: a good CEO should make a good company. Unattainable and unrealistic expectations are aroused.

The future is not always rewarded with the sweet-smelling flowers of success, however. There is internal dissatisfaction, combined with bruised egos and disappointed expectation. There is institutionalized friction and resistance to change. There may also be a hemorrhage of some of the firm's best people. The new CEO has probably been called a superstar so many times that he starts to believe it. This causes communications problems. He might not realize that the chalice is poisoned.

Khurana's most recent research has retained its concentration on management personnel. It has shifted to examine the professionalization of management alongside medicine, architecture, or law. Sociologists have long agreed that managers are very near the top of the social pile: they earn good salaries and enjoy social respect and deference. But, unlike other professions, there is no ritualized process of professionalization that can certify the inductee as a member. There is no professional body of management entitling members to act or practice exclusively as managers. It is true that the M.B.A. qualification, earned from one of the better B-schools, has become increasingly necessary for entry into management; however, this is not rigidly exclusive.

Essential reading

http://rakeshkhurana.typepad.com/about.html

Searching for a Corporate Savior: The Irrational Search for Charismatic CEOs (Princeton University Press, 2002)

W. CHAN KIM AND RENÉE MAUBORGNE

Educators (2005 Ranking: 15)

W. Chan Kim is The Boston Consulting Group Bruce D. Henderson Chair Professor of Strategy and International Management at INSEAD Business School, France. Prior to joining the INSEAD faculty, he was a professor at the University of Michigan Business School. Renée Mauborgne is Distinguished Fellow and affiliate Professor of Strategy and Management, also at INSEAD.

Their recent publication, *Blue Ocean Strategy* (2005), is a summation of a decade of articles on value innovation, including one in the *Harvard Business Review*. Kim and Mauborgne have presented themselves as unashamed strategic iconoclasts. The thinking behind most business strategy sees the agents as either individual companies or industries as a whole. The scene for strategic activity is essentially fixed and finite. Analogies were often made with the field of battle or the theater of war. Some strategists went further in borrowing military symbols. They talked about headquarters rather than the corporate head office. The battlefield was fixed in area; no new land could be added to it or created. Any struggles that took place were zero-sum games. These conflicts were intense and bloody (in figurative terms), staining red the ground on which they were fought.

Anecdotal evidence pointed to a different, non-static commercial battlefield. Industries and businesses grow up, while others decay. Kim and Mauborgne established a historical database of businesses. This showed that very few of the industries in existence in the first decade of the twentieth century were still in the picture a century later. Their research also showed that new industries are being created at a phenomenal rate, far faster than ever before. Where is the finite theater of battle, they ask? The world is not stained red from the blood of conflict. There are vast areas of "blue ocean" to be tapped. According to Kim and Mauborgne, there is a huge and underestimated capacity to create new industries. Most strategists seem, at best, ambivalent about this.

The successful industries of today were unheard of 30 years ago. A similar pattern can, with confidence, be projected into the future. The only certainty is that most industries are important at some time, but no industry remains great forever; the same can be said about companies. This demonstrates the unsuitability of companies and industries as subjects for strategic inquiry. These patterns have nothing to do with business cycles. "The moment you take an industry-deterministic view of your company you are a victim of that industry."

There is no reason why, with a bold and creative approach, declines cannot be halted and turned around. What matters most are "smart strategic moves." The most important of these is the creation and capturing of new market space. To return to the earlier analogy, new land is needed. This reclamation is affected by strategic moves. These are "the actions of players in conceiving, launching, and realizing business ideals." Kim and Mauborgne give a number of examples. The introduction of the Model T by Ford in 1908 was a strategic move *par excellence*. It launched the American auto industry and catapulted Ford to a predominant market share. When, in 1924, General Motors launched its cars "for every purpose and every purse," it knocked Ford out of the box, soon gaining a 50 percent market share. This was also a strategic move. It revitalized the auto industry. Both Ford and then GM achieved value innovation. The secret to success is realizing what are the smart and strategic moves. As the experience of Ford and many others shows, strategic moves can and often are copied eventually. Those seeking azure-blue seas must be aware that, sooner or later, they will be dyed blood red as the forces of corporate competition take them over.

While that may be inevitable, it should not stop the search for value innovation. What Kim and Mauborgne are telling business is to forget about the old stresses. Don't try fighting in territory that is contested; find a new market. Stop worrying about the competition – make it irrelevant. This way it is possible to offer lower prices *and* a differentiated product or service.

Value innovation is a function of strategy. Another important notion of contemporary business is "fair process." This is a vital part of successful management. It involves recognition of employees through engagement. Its aim is to gain the emotional and intellectual commitment of employees who are a company's single greatest asset.

Essential reading

http://www.blueoceanstrategy.com
Blue Ocean Strategy: How to Create Uncontested Market Space and Make the Competition Irrelevant (Harvard Business School Press, 2005)

NAOMI KLEIN
Journalist (2005 Ranking: 46)

Naomi Klein (born 1970) is a Canadian journalist and author. She is best known for her book *No Logo: Taking Aim at the Brand Bullies* (2000), an examination of anti-corporate activism throughout the world. This has been called "the *Das Kapital* of the anti-globalization movement." The book has already been translated into 16 languages.

Klein also writes regularly for the Toronto *Globe and Mail* newspaper in Canada and *The Guardian* in the U.K. Apart from her writing activities, Klein has lectured at Harvard, Yale, and New York University.

In her youth, Klein was obsessed with brands and logos, like those of McDonald's and Shell. She thought if she could climb on to the fluorescent signs it would be "like touching something from another dimension." This was translated during her teenage years into an obsession for designer clothes. She was described in high school as the pupil most likely to end up in jail.

She went from the brands' greatest fan to their most trenchant critic in the book *No Logo*.

Logos and brands have become a forceful international language, understood and recognized by billions. They are everywhere, even on the space station. We are being united by what we are being sold. However, the means of advertising have become more pervasive. No longer content with magazines, billboards, or television, some companies are using nifty new tricks. Young people are being targeted at schools and colleges.

Brands find the Internet to be an El Dorado. Free of the traditional burdens of shops and factories they are "...free to soar, less as the disseminators of goods or services than as collective hallucinations." The companies behind them offer a commitment to multicultural diversity. This is a sham: it only creates more buying and selling opportunities. In their domination and re-creation of taste, they practice censorship, so that they are not just dominating the world, they are shaping its mindset as well.

Logos and brands have a very harmful impact on many of the world's societies, be they producers or consumers. Klein looks in detail at the status of workers for some of these corporations, quoting a senior executive who described the idea of a "living wage" for some employees as "romantically appealing" but no more. She also writes about the increasing use of "perma-temps" or workers who have very responsible jobs but are not allowed any of the benefits of permanent workers like pensions and healthcare benefits. Her book was taken up as a rallying cry by hosts of young people who had previously had no interest in politics or movements. The British band Radiohead banned logos from their gigs after reading her book.

Apart from giving a voice to the anti-corporate movement, she also describes it. Unlike other movements, it is noticeable for its lack of clear organization and traditional leadership. It appears anarchic. What leadership exists is likely to be ephemeral, provided by pop stars. These people are often applying their own carefully crafted brand image. These happenings are characterized by "grass roots" movements. The book was very popular with people in search of something to believe in, although it was patently one-sided. It was also the work of a very good journalist – someone who can bring facts into view – but there was little analysis or theory beyond a simplistic anti-capitalism.

Her next book, *Fences and Windows* (2001), was never meant to be a follow-up to *No Logo*. It is a collection of articles on the anti-globalization movement since the World Trade Organization Summit in Seattle in 2001. Klein describes the battles between the police and protesters as "an activist model that mirrors the organic decentralized pathways of the Internet – the Internet come to life."

Many of Naomi Klein's articles and dispatches, as well as answers to questions such as "How can I consume ethically?" are available on her website.

Essential reading

http://www.nologo.org

No Logo: Taking Aim at the Brand Bullies (Vintage Canada, 2000)

Fences and Windows: Dispatches From the Front Lines of the Globalization Debate (Vintage Canada, 2001)

PHILIP KOTLER

Educator (2005 Ranking: 7)

Philip Kotler (born 1931) is the S. C. Johnson Distinguished Professor of International Marketing at the J. L. Kellogg Graduate School of Management, Northwestern University. Apart from his teaching and writing, Kotler has worked as a marketing consultant to many of America's top companies.

Although his name is now inseparable from marketing, Kotler trained as an economist. He gained a masters degree from the University of Chicago and a doctorate from the Massachusetts Institute of Technology. He returned to Chicago to complete post-doctoral research in behavioral sciences, as well as undertaking research in mathematics at Harvard.

When it comes to marketing, Professor Kotler wrote *the* book on the subject. His *Marketing Management: Application, Planning, Implementation and Control* (1967), now in its twelfth edition, is the core text of marketing courses in most M.B.A. programs.

Peter Drucker was the first to urge management to take marketing seriously. It was not just a fancy form of salesmanship, but one of the most important company functions (along with innovation). Before Kotler marketing was synonymous with the marketing mix and the four Ps (product, pricing, place, and promotion). As the marketing concept became much broader, the four Ps had to be redefined too. Central to the book is the need for companies to actively create and nurture markets. "Good companies will meet needs; great companies will create markets," he noted.

This involved areas such as marketing planning, market research, and customer relationship management. Kotler has written that marketing is vital to "value creation and raising the world's living standards." It is "meeting needs profitably." He has always tried to expand discussions about marketing beyond production and service provision. He has written books on the marketing of places, ideas, and celebrities (*High Visibility*, 1987). He has also produced works for specialist audiences like not-for-profit organizations, religious congregations, even museums. He believes that the most satisfying marketing job in the world is bringing "more health and education to people and making a real difference in their quality of life."

The business world has changed a lot since *Marketing Management* was first published. The nature of the four Ps had undergone transformation. Kotler considers that they are still important building blocks, but that each one has developed its own subset of tools. Instead of just a marketing mix, there is a pricing mix, a positioning mix, and so on. Markets and media have become more sophisticated. The power of brands has grown. So too have the means by which producers and providers can create awareness. Marketing is now a global activity. The world of marketing is dynamic.

Kotler has conducted research into the impact of the Internet on the marketing concept and examines this in one of his latest books, *Marketing Moves* (2002). He talks about holistic marketing: "… where a company combines the informational power of enterprise resource planning, supply chain management, and customer relationship management to leverage greater success in the marketplace." This often leads to collaborative networks using the Internet, corporate intranets, and extranets to achieve growth. It is holistic because it no longer sees marketing as a discrete, department-bound activity. It must become "the architect of the company's demand-and-supply chain and its network of collaborators."

Marketing has to be at the center of business activity. It must concentrate on customers: "Customer focus is critical in a world no longer marked by a shortage of goods but by a shortage of customers." He has looked at companies like Amazon.com. It initially seemed to possess great competitive advantage because it did not have huge physical assets. It had to spend huge amounts on marketing to build its brand and retain customer loyalty. Kotler also believes that "M-marketing," using mobile devices like mobile phones, will grow in importance. Marketing managers will have to develop skills in:

- Database management and data mining
- Partnership relationship management
- Telemarketing and call-center management
- Customization of offerings, services, and messages
- Experiential marketing

He also foresees marketing managers having access to "real-time" information dashboards. This will allow them to track prices, costs, and sales of individual products in real time.

Essential reading

http://www.kotlermarketing.com/resources/philipkotler.html
Principles of Marketing (Prentice Hall, 1999)
Social Marketing: Improving the Quality of Life (Free Press, 2002)
Marketing Moves: A New Approach to Profits, Growth and Renewal (Harvard Business School Press, 2002)
Marketing Management: Application, Planning, Implementation and Control (1967); 12th edition (Prentice Hall, 2005) (with Kevin Keller)

PAUL KRUGMAN
Economist and Columnist
(2005 Ranking: 39)

Paul Krugman (born 1953) is Professor of Economics and International Affairs at Princeton. He is a native of New York's Long Island. In his youth he dreamed of becoming a "psychohistorian" *à la* Isaac Asimov: someone who could predict the future. Disabused of such ideals, he studied economics at Yale, and received a doctorate from M.I.T. – probably the nearest equivalent. He subsequently taught at both institutions as well as at Stanford. He is recognized among economists as a doyen of the New Trade Theory. This theory seeks to overturn the traditional notions of international trade, still rooted in Ricardian Comparative Advantage. Technology is driving and molding world trade.

Krugman worked briefly on the Council of Economic Advisers. Most politicians have considered him too volatile to serve for long in high-profile public roles. He has attacked the domination of policy entrepreneurs – unqualified hacks whose policies and decisions are motivated by short-term electoral spin – in all administrations. These people "… repeat silly clichés but imagine themselves to be sophisticated."

While he has earned the respect of his fellow economists, he is better known to a wider world through his books and writings. The first was *The Age of Diminished Expectations* (1994). *Peddling Prosperity* (1994) was an attack on the policy entrepreneurs behind much of the Clinton Administration's economic policy. From the mid 1990s Krugman has collected many of his shorter pieces and articles into books like *Pop Internationalism* (1996) and *The*

Accidental Theorist (1999), subtitled (somewhat tongue-in-cheek) *Dispatches from the Dismal Science*. There are also his widely read and widely syndicated op-ed pieces in *The New York Times* and his writing for such popular magazines as *Fortune* and *Slate*.

The Return of Depression Economics (1999) was written at the height of sustained economic, mainly technology-driven, growth. It sounded a commonsensical warning – what goes up must … This was backed up by examination of the fragility of economic success, especially that in Southeast Asia, which had been brought to a painful though temporary halt by the currency crises of 1997.

With the moral certitude of an economist he has poured criticism on the economic policies of many countries, including France and Japan. However, he has directed his most forceful ire towards his homeland.

Krugman has become a trenchant critic of the economic policies of the Bush Administration. These criticisms are collected in *The Great Unraveling* (2003). He describes how bullishness was replaced by bearishness and how the world of the corporate hero was replaced by the world of corporate sleaze, caused by Enron and other scandal-hit firms. He lays the blame for this change at the door of George W. Bush: "First, use cooked numbers to justify big giveaways to the top. Then if things don't work out, let ordinary workers who trusted you pay the price."

Along with Alan Greenspan, he is the most influential economist in the U.S. today. He shows that the pen is still mightier than a lot of offensive hardware. Yet these economists owe their power to the media that convey their message. Krugman hardly ever strays far from his academic base in Princeton. He does not run a consultancy either.

He is in favor of globalization as it is potentially beneficial to the whole world. He brands much of the criticism directed against it as self-righteous "globaloney." He castigates those who still believe protectionism has a role to play in modern economics. In spite of his belief in a new world order in trade, he is skeptical of the impact of technology on modern life, seeing some of the comments as little more than hype. The new global economy has not made traditional economic theory redundant, he says. He is also dismissive of supply-siders who believe tax cuts, especially those based on fuzzy math, are the answer to everything. This is a "crank doctrine" appealing to the preju-

dices of rich men and women that offers "self-esteem to the intellectually insecure." Monopolistic competition and "crony capitalism" are also targets.

He believes in the intellectual purity of economics as a discipline. All too
often, economics attracts charlatans and latter-day snake-oil salesmen, he
says. Economics may not be rocket science, but it is still a science, though
maybe not a dismal one.

Essential reading

http://www.wws.princeton.edu/pkrugman/

*Peddling Prosperity: Economic Sense and Nonsense in the Age of Diminished
Expectations* (WW Norton, 1994)

The Age of Diminished Expectations: U.S. Economic Policy in the 1990s (MIT
Press, 1994)

The Return of Depression Economics (WW Norton, 1999)

The Great Unraveling: From Boom to Bust in Three Scandalous Years (WW
Norton, 2003)

COSTAS MARKIDES
Educator (2005 Ranking: 49)

Constantinos C. Markides is Robert P. Bauman Professor of Strategic Leadership at London Business School. Born in Cyprus in 1960, he studied economics at Boston University, earning a masters degree. He subsequently received an M.B.A. and D.B.A. from Harvard Business School.

Markides has made a number of contributions to strategic management thinking. In "To Diversify Or Not To Diversify?" (a 1997 *Harvard Business Review* article) he discussed some key questions tied to business diversification. Should companies diversify? What does that mean? Should a company move fast or slow in its diversification? To address such questions, he pointed to a number of success stories, including the Canadian company Bombardier, which started out during World War II as a producer of vehicles for snow-covered terrain. By the 1990s, it was one of the world's biggest manufacturers of buses and watercraft. Markides illustrates how Bombardier's successful diversification was a slow and cautious affair. It might also be argued that it wasn't really diversification at all, just a stretching of their initial emphasis on specialized transport vehicles. For Bombardier the rewards for its diversification were considerable, but such rewards do not come to everyone, especially if they make the wrong investment calls, says Markides.

As a specialist in strategy and someone with Greek roots, Markides is aware that *strategy* comes from the Greek verb "to lead." Strategy, therefore, involves dynamism and movement. In *All the Right Moves* (1999) he proffers the view that successful business strategy should focus on asking (and finding the answers to) three fundamental questions:

* Who should I target as customers?
* What products or services should I offer them?
* How can I do this in an efficient way?

But finding a successful strategy is also about creativity. Business leaders should consider stretching their strategic muscles by asking questions from offbeat or unorthodox angles. Perhaps the poorest way to manage strategic decision-making, he argues, is the classic corporate mode of producing mountains of data and analyzing it *ad infinitum* hoping that salient answers to the key questions will somehow evolve. Markides also cautions that a successful strategy is volatile and often has a short shelf life. Just because a strategy worked for your company yesterday doesn't mean it will work tomorrow. Thus, leaders must know the right strategy moves but just as importantly know how to deploy a strategy creatively. It is also important to know when to break the rules of the game.

In *Fast Second* (co-authored with Paul Geroski in 2004), Markides uses the metaphor of a landscape to describe the business world. There are new areas to be explored. This is done by people and organizations he terms "colonists." These are the firms that routinely take risks, face dangers and uncertainties, and often have to come up with new and innovative approaches to survival. In business terms, these are the people who make breakthroughs in any area – whether technology, pharmaceuticals, or even service providers. But colonists are generally hopeless at bringing the fruits of their efforts to market.

For marketplace success, bigger organizations with a different mindset are needed. These are the "consolidators." They scale up the breakthroughs of the colonists and make them fit for consumers to consume. The two kinds of businesses are like different species; rare, if not unknown, is the organization that can do both. The colonists are good at being colonists, not at being consolidators. And vice versa.

But this paradigm isn't appreciated. Many consolidator organizations enviously eye the colonists with their efficiencies and their zest for success. They sometimes attempt to become more entrepreneurial, or they set up incubators, or they announce that they are "going back to the garage." Such attempts, Markides believes, are futile. Such attempts reveal, minimally, a sense of corporate arrogance – maybe even corporate hubris. Consolidators should realize their advantages and be content to capitalize on them. One of these is a first-in-the-market advantage, allied to but separate from first-mover advantage. Colonists are the best first movers, but they're unable to make much market success. Ultimately, large-scale success belongs to the organization that can bring an idea to the market in a big way. Consolidators should be more than happy to be fast seconds because they are emulating the likes of corporate brethren such as Microsoft and Canon.

Essential reading

http://forum.london.edu/lbsbiogs.nsf/(httpBiographiesBySurnameSearch)/markides

Diversification, Refocusing, and Economic Performance (MIT Press, 1996)

"To Diversify or Not to Diversify?" *Harvard Business Review*, November–December 1997, pp. 93–99

All the Right Moves: A Guide to Crafting Breakthrough Strategy (Harvard Business School Press, 1999)

Fast Second: How Smart Companies Bypass Radical Innovation to Enter and Dominate New Markets (Jossey-Bass, 2004) (with Paul A. Geroski)

HENRY MINTZBERG
Educator (2005 Ranking: 8)

Henry Mintzberg (born 1939) is a management strategist "in spite of himself." He is Cleghorne Professor of Management Studies at McGill University in Canada and is also a faculty member of France's prestigious INSEAD. His involvement with B-schools is somewhat paradoxical, given his strident attacks on their training methods, structure, and (as he would see it) pretensions.

He studied mechanical engineering at Toronto's McGill University before earning his Ph.D. at the Massachusetts Institute of Technology's Sloan School of Management. He has written 15 books and many articles and papers.

Mintzberg first came to a wider public with his book *The Nature of Managerial Work* (1973), based on his doctoral research. He asked 25 senior executives to keep diaries noting their work. He also interviewed them continually. Mintzberg honed in on a big discrepancy. The managers told him their activities were governed by traditional management tasks like planning, organizing, commanding, co-ordinating, and controlling, yet their diaries revealed no such commitment to theories. Most decisions were made off the cuff in an almost instinctive way. When it came to information, they placed most credence in what they had just heard.

In *Structures in Fives* (1983) he wrote that formal barriers and functional frontiers should be abolished. Hierarchies were outdated. The best way to get things done was through informal, amorphous teams. These would change their membership frequently and would even change their terms of reference as old problems declined in importance and new ones emerged. This "blobby" environment he termed an "adhocracy" to distinguish it from a bureaucracy.

All this undermines the need for rigid strategy. Never a shrinking violet, Mintzberg pronounced its present death in *The Rise and Fall of Strategic Planning* (2000). It is bound to fail, as it is a unity of opposites: strategy is about synthesis, planning about analysis. Strategy has often destroyed commitment and distorted vision. There is still a need, though, for informal learning and the harnessing of personal vision.

Mintzberg has been critical of management education, especially M.B.A. programs: "M.B.A. schools train the wrong people in the wrong way for the wrong reasons." His attitude towards those holding the precious three-letter suffix is stark. He once said that they should carry a tattooed skull-and-cross-bones on their foreheads, above the legend "Not prepared to manage." His criticisms are contained in *Managers Not MBAs* (2004): "You cannot learn to lead an organization from a classroom." Leadership and management are not separate. His criticism embraces some of the goliaths of international management education. They want to turn management into a science or a profession, forgetting about its emotional and often less rational aspects. He sees management as a craft: "It's as much about doing in order to think, as about thinking in order to do."

B-schools teach business functions, not management. They inculcate a narrow-minded and mercenary outlook, combined with a lack of social awareness. Their products are usually groomed to look on their employees as resources instead of people. He is also highly critical of much management consultancy. Traditional M.B.A. graduates are like a virus, destroying management practice from the inside, and at the same time blinding companies to other types of management and alternative ways of training managers. Rather than throw fireballs from the sidelines Mintzberg developed his own programs at McGill such as the International Masters in Practicing Management (IMPM), designed for those who already know something of management in the world's top companies.

Companies have been suborned to the interests of large shareholders, which causes widespread corporate social irresponsibility. Mintzberg also believes that many of the corporate social responsibility initiatives are window dressing. Any attempt to be more socially responsive or ethical is inevitably stymied by a need for the company's stock to perform well.

He is not reticent about directing his spleen at specific industries, like the world's airlines. These are mercilessly pilloried in *Why I Hate Flying* (2001) – he does not mind flying: it is airlines and airports he hates. They say they are motivated by the highest standards of management and promise comfort. In practice, air travel is an ordeal, whether for those in "sardine" or "pampered" class. However, he argues much of this is planned. Customer loyalty and frequent-flyer schemes are often scams, in which travelers are bribed with their own money.

Essential reading

http://www.henrymintzberg.com/
The Nature of Managerial Work (Harper & Row, 1973)
Structures in Fives: Designing Effective Organizations (Prentice Hall, 1983)
The Rise and Fall of Strategic Planning (Free Press, 1994)
Why I Hate Flying: Tales for the Tormented Traveler (Thompson, 2001)
Managers Not MBAs (Financial Times Prentice Hall, 2004)

GEOFFREY MOORE
Consultant (2005 Ranking: 50)

Geoff Moore brought marketing into the cyber age although his first calling was English literature. He earned his primary degree from Stanford and a Ph.D. from the University of Washington. He taught for a while as a professor at Olivet College, Michigan, but he subsequently undertook a major career revision, entering the world of marketing high-technology products. He eventually became a partner in the marketing strategy firm Regis McKenna Inc. He then established his own marketing consultancy, Chasm Group (named after his first book). He is also a partner in the California venture capital firm Mohr Davidow.

His experience in marketing high-tech products had taught him that traditional marketing procedures were increasingly inapplicable. He identified a technology adaptation life cycle (TALC). A new piece of hardware or software may be truly revolutionary in what it can do. Its promise is recognized and taken up by technologically savvy customers who do not need spoon-feeding on how to use it. However, once this relatively small market has been satisfied, sales go into a hole. Mainstream buyers simply don't want to know about the product: they are unsure about it. They may see it as just too fancy and complicated. Some of this springs from inertia and a fear of the new. Moore also recognizes a quite rational worry about congruence and compatibility issues. There are hardcore technophobes as well, some still inhabiting caves.

In *Crossing the Chasm* (1991) Moore sought to show technology companies how they could make it to the other side of the chasm. The compatibility issues could be addressed by developers producing fully integrated products and suites. He advises informed caution, however; technology companies should do their homework. They should identify key segments in their target markets and work assiduously towards acceptance. Much of Moore's theory is based on the Social Proof in Influence paradigm. This teaches that a new technology (or anything new) is adopted first by pragmatic people and organizations. Their example is then copied by other pragmatists. It is important to get these people, the early majority, on board as customers. As pragmatists they want solutions, the easier to apply, the better. Then there is the late majority – the people who wait. They are unsure of the world around them and hold out until new technology standards have been established. After a fair dose of cutthroat competition has reduced prices, they eventually buy into the technology.

Inside the Tornado (1995) was written as a sequel for those who had jumped successfully across the chasm. Moore illustrates how some companies have coped with success in a mass-market environment. TALC is still an issue: companies must test how ready their customers are for their technology. Many of the thought processes that have led to a successful journey over the chasm may have to be unlearned and set aside.

The Gorilla Game (1998) was a joint effort, written with marketing strategist Tom Kippola and investment analyst Paul Johnson. It aimed to marry much of the method of *Crossing the Chasm* to the world of investment in high-tech companies, at the time the hottest of stocks.

Moore's most recent book, *Living on the Fault Line* (2000), is not (in spite of its title) a memoir of life in the San Francisco area. It is written for the management of publicly quoted technology companies that have been established for some time. They have catapulted the chasm, survived the tornado, and yet are still looking for signposts. They are under attack by new, disruptive technologies. They know they have to keep up, but they seldom know where or how to run. The book provides some answers and models to pursue.

Essential reading

http://www.tcg-advisors.com/who/moore.htm
Crossing the Chasm: Marketing and Selling Technology Products to Mainstream Customers (Collins, 1991, revised 1999)

Inside the Tornado: Marketing Strategies from Silicon Valley's Cutting Edge (Collins, 1995, revised 2004)

The Gorilla Game: Investor's Guide to Picking Winners in High Technology (Collins, 1998) (with Tom Kippola and Paul Johnson)

Living on the Fault Line: Managing for Shareholder Value in the Age of the Internet (Collins, 2000)

KJELL NORDSTRÖM AND JONAS RIDDERSTRÅLE

Educators (2005 Ranking: 9)

Kjell Nordström and Jonas Ridderstråle are both professors at the Stockholm School of Economics: Nordström at the Institute of International Business, Ridderstråle at the Centre for Advanced Studies in Leadership. They both hold doctorates in international business and economics and are highly respected members of the Swedish academic family. Both consult to Swedish and international companies and have a broad range of business interests.

They have achieved fame among the ranks of management thinkers through their books and their lectures, both of which are different. At their lectures (they prefer to call them "gigs") they appear (should that be perform?) together, dressed in black. The similarities with the world of rock music are deliberate. Their delivery is fast and punchy. Another flamboyant presenter, Tom Peters (a big fan), might be described as a modern country-and-western performer; these guys are definitely hard-core heavy metal *artistes.*

Their first book, *Funky Business* (1999), caught the atmosphere of their gigs. It contained some stark and simple messages. The world of business has changed dramatically. What will work has to be different in a revolutionary way:

Traditional roles, jobs, skills, ways of doing things, insights, strategies, aspirations, fears and expectations no longer count … We cannot have business as usual. We need business as unusual. We need different business. We need innovative business. We need unpredictable business. We need surprising business. We need funky business.

The successful organizations will be different, too, unafraid of difference or creativity: *They will seek emotion.* The meaning of e-commerce must be changed to emotional commerce. Employees should be hired because they have some of that emotion. They can then be trained to carry out specific skills. They should be sought in unusual ways, even at pop concerts, far removed from the traditional hiring venues.

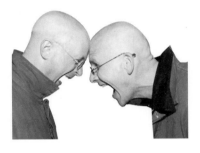

Ideas are what will make a difference. Riches should be sought in niches, wherever they are, among "homosexual dentists or pigeon-fancying lawyers."

The workplace of the future will be *Funky Inc.* It "isn't like any other company … [It] thrives on the changing circumstances and unpredictability of our times." The future will be incoherent, dominated by movement and speed, by the imperatives of "move it, move it fast, move it faster, move it now." The strengths of an organization will not be core competencies but core *competents*, people whose skills and knowledge make a difference: "These walking monopolies will stay as long as the company offers them something they want. When that is no longer the case they will leave."

Today's world is a place of excess. This is the age of time and talent, both of which are commodities. Talent will allow firms to be unique. The challenge is: How are *you* making yourself more attractive, more sexy? In a world of economic Darwinism, survival is a question of being either fit or sexy. Competition takes place using models and moods. Fitness boils down to using market imperfections to your advantage. Masters of mood exploit the imperfections of man by seducing or sedating the consumer. Excellent companies reinvent innovation.

Their second book, *Karaoke Capitalism* (2004), was never going to be a dog-eared sequel to their earlier volume, a mere *"Funky 2."* The two Swedes attempted to address political and ideological issues and to ask what changes we can expect to emerge from a world dominated by super-fast and soulless machines. In places the book reads like a manifesto, a call to the barricades. The world is undergoing change on a scale unknown before, greater than the move from an agricultural to an industrial society that took place in Europe 200 years ago. That took well over a century and was accompanied by major changes in behavior and religious observance as well as political changes. Individuals now have more choice than ever. The world of *Karaoke Capitalism* is increasingly dominated by copycats bashing out cover versions of great originals. Only imagination, innovation, and originality will place societies, organizations, and individuals center stage. The book talks about how to create capitalism with character and how to live a fulfilling life while making a living. To develop the character of capitalism involves accepting individual responsibility: "Look inside. Do you want to be a first-rate version of yourself or a second-rate version of someone else?"

Both books are written in an uncompromising style. Sometimes they deliberately aim below the belt and between the eyes.

Essential reading

http://www.funkybusiness.com
http://www.karaokecapitalism.com
Funky Business (Financial Times Prentice Hall, 1999)
Karaoke Capitalism: Managing for Mankind (Praeger, 2004)

KENICHI OHMAE
Consultant (2005 Ranking: 16)

Kenichi Ohmae (born 1943) studied at Waseda University before going to the Massachusetts Institute of Technology, where he gained a Ph.D. in nuclear engineering. On returning to Japan, he worked initially on the implementation of the country's nuclear power program, before joining McKinsey & Company. He has wide-ranging interests in a host of issues, from the world economy to the problems besetting Japan. He founded a political movement and stood unsuccessfully for the governorship of Tokyo. He has written a vast number of books and papers and is dean of two business schools in Tokyo in which he also teaches. He has taught at Stanford as well as on an innovative e-learning M.B.A. taught by Bond University in Australia. He has numerous businesses in Japan, including a television channel, Business Breakthrough TV.

Strategy, for Ohmae, has always had a lot to do with intuition. It helps those who use it wisely to see clearly. In *The Mind of the Strategist* (1982) he explained the reasons behind the success of some Japanese companies.

Ohmae was aware that the world was changing. Improvements in telecommunications were shrinking distances and creating new possibilities. In *Triad Power* (1985) he identified three concentrations of wealth in the world. Companies had to compete globally if they were to succeed. This meant entering all triad markets simultaneously.

Ohmae viewed the persistence of national borders as a restriction on the flow of goods and information. Borders exist to buttress the outdated concept of the nation-state. They have been stripped of much of their power by the rise of the Internet. The future lies in groupings of nations coming together for economic reasons, like the European Union.

In *The Invisible Continent* (2000) Ohmae continues his exploration of success in the new global economy. The companies that will succeed owe much to pursuing the right strategy, but this is often informed by intuition. These companies have something equivalent to a genetic fingerprint for global success. He terms them "Godzilla" companies.

In *The Next Global Stage* (2005) he reassesses the global economy that has been created by improved telecommunications. He eschews the term "new economy": it has been degraded by association with a narrow concentration on growth and productivity during the dot.com era. It was based on new trading concepts such as the greater use of multiples in assessing companies' worth. The world was in a state of super-liquidity. The key to tapping into that liquidity was to attract it. The lodestone of attraction was no longer the nation-state but the investor-friendly region. There was no need for a region to be based on any pre-existing geographical unit. It did not have to have any natural resources. It should have good technical and intellectual infrastructure, but it did not need any traditional natural resources to achieve prosperity. It could be resource-poor in traditional economic terms, but it could easily overcome this by possessing sufficient knowledge workers. It did not matter how poor it was: the secret to prosperity was to attract wealth from the ROW (Rest of the World). This then led to specialization. An example of a once poor region that successfully attracted inward investment is Ireland. It had realized quite early that wealth in the Information Age came at the end of a telephone line.

Another aspect of the global economy is the existence of platforms. These are agreed-upon technical standards enabling easy communication. They range from the communications platform of the English language, whose use has become predominant in the business world, to IT standards such as the Internet protocol. The U.S. dollar has the status of a monetary platform, used for transactions and savings by people with no ties or links to the United States.

Along with the connectivity provided by telecommunications and computer science advances, the global economy is facilitated daily by improvements in logistics. Goods can be assembled and distributed easily by the same company or through a strategic partnership.

The global economy is a place of shifting sands. Old industries are dying with amazing speed; new ones are taking their place. But certainties are few. An industry leader has to accept that it could easily find itself in a leading or prominent position in a completely different industry. It has to cope with this loss of orientation.

The greatest dangers in the global economy are old-style paradigms, such as the nation-state and protectionist mentalities.

Essential reading

http://www.kohmae.com

Triad Power: The Coming Shape of Global Competition (Free Press, 1985)

The Borderless World: Power and Strategy in the Interlinked Economy (Harper Business, 1990)

The End of the Nation State: The Rise of Regional Economies (Harper Collins, 1995)

The Invisible Continent: Global Strategy in the New Economy (Harper Business, 2000)

The Next Global Stage: The Challenges and Opportunities in Our Borderless World (Wharton, 2005)

DON PEPPERS
Consultant (2005 Ranking: 38)

Don Peppers is a co-founder of Peppers & Rogers, a customer-focused management consultancy. Peppers is regarded as the father of the customer relationship management (CRM) phenomenon.

He earned a degree in aeronautical engineering from the U.S. Air Force Academy and a masters degree in public affairs from Princeton's Woodrow Wilson School. He worked for a U.S. regional airline prior to entering the world of marketing and advertising, becoming CEO of Perkins/Butler Direct Marketing Inc. He eventually founded Peppers & Rogers with his collaborator and co-author Martha Rogers. The firm, with offices on six continents, is now part of the Carlson Marketing Group.

To paraphrase George Orwell, customers are equal, but some are more equal than others. Peppers aims to show through his work on customer relationship management that some customers are more profitable than others while some are dead losses. A company can make a lot of money by identifying the former and discarding the latter. Anyone in business lucky enough to have lots of customers, be they a multinational or mom-and-pop store, will have their favorite customers as well as those whom they wish would take their custom elsewhere. This sums up a good deal of Peppers' management ideas. Hunches and feelings must be replaced by more scientific methods of identifying the wheat from the chaff.

For Peppers there are three types of customers:

+ Most Valuable Customers (MVCs): These can be shown, mathematically, to contribute to profit. Each transaction is profitable. Maybe it involves buying an item or service with a good margin or is a transaction leading to other transactions. The MVCs keep coming back. They are serial profit providers. They do not eat into staff time, and they do not tie up resources with vexatious complaints.
+ Most Growable Customers (MGCs): These may be new customers. Some high-powered computer-aided number crunching can confirm that they are profitable now or that they are potentially profitable in the not-too-distant future.
+ The "Below-Zeroes": These customers cost the firm more than they provide. Either they are low-volume buyers in low-margin areas, or they are perennially finding fault, holding up staff with trivial complaints, or possibly sending items back with demands for refunds.

Knowing who falls into the MVC category is useful. Resources can be directed towards servicing their business and keeping them. There can be positively discriminated interaction with them. Time and resources can be devoted to greater customization of the products or services sought by MVCs. Their queries and complaints can be fast-tracked for speedy resolution. In fact, with caller identification of telephone numbers, any communication from them can be responded to quickly and efficiently, instead of their being put on hold.

Peppers and Rogers extended their analysis from "one-to-one" business–customer interfaces to B2B (or business-to-business contacts) in *One to One B2B* (2001). There was the same tripartite customer profile and a similar need to keep good customers. Further research found that business MVCs had things in common, like a stable management team, as well as having shared corporate values.

As a company gets to know MVCs better, it can anticipate their needs better and their loyalty can be rewarded. The logic is that the MVCs and MGCs should be pursued at the expense of the Below-Zero people, who should be discarded.

Essential reading

http://www.1to1.com/View.aspx?BioID=9493

The One to One Future (Currency, 1993) (with Martha Rogers)

One to One B2B: Customer Development Strategies for the Business-to-Business World (Currency, 2001) (with Martha Rogers)

Life's a Pitch: How to Outwit Your Competitors and Make a Winning Presentation (Currency, 2002)

Managing Customer Relationships: A Strategic Framework (Wiley, 2004) (with Martha Rogers)

TOM PETERS
Consultant (2005 Ranking: 4)

....

Tom Peters (born 1942) is a native of Baltimore. He studied engineering at Cornell before heading to the west coast to get his M.B.A. and Ph.D. at Stanford. He saw active service in the Vietnam War with the U.S. Navy. In the mid 1970s he joined McKinsey as a consultant, leaving in 1981 to set up his own firm, now part of the Tom Peters Group.

In Search of Excellence appeared in 1982 (co-written with Robert Waterman, a fellow McKinsey partner). This became the best-selling management book of the twentieth century – the first to reach the best-seller charts. This was soon followed by the nearly-as-successful *A Passion for Excellence* (1985).

Excellence has achieved a cult following. It tied in with the need in the early 1980s to feel good again about being American. It showed that significant parts of American industry and business *were* excellent; others could be too. Its simplistic rhetoric earned Peters a rap on the knuckles from the venerable Peter Drucker, who chided Peters for making "managing sound so incredibly easy. All you have to do is put that book under your pillow and it will get done."

In Search of Excellence is an American classic. It contains great stories of do-and-dare about 43 excellent American companies; it is not long on theorizing. It is liberally spiced with nuggets of homespun wisdom: "If a window of opportunity appears, don't pull down the shade."

According to the book, excellence in business depends on eight factors:

+ Promote people who "do it, fix it [and] try it"
+ Learn from the people you serve (the customers)

 * Encourage entrepreneurship and autonomy
 * Take a "hands-on" approach
 * Value workers as the key to productivity
 * Stick to the knitting, exploit your core competencies
 * Keep your organization simple and your staff lean
 * Utilize simultaneously loose–tight controls

Peters has always been in favor of delegation in a company. The manager cannot know everything. If he tries, he will get snowed under in useless detail.

A Darwinian approach to the achievement of excellence had to be adopted to achieve excellence. It is better to do something wrong than do nothing: people should not be terrified of making mistakes. The next time they try, they'll learn from it and do it right, or hopefully better. Therefore, excellence can be gained incrementally, through a series of small steps bonded by a central message.

Peters is not a captive to consistency. A lot of the excellent companies praised by him in *Excellence* have not stood the test of corporate time. Some have disappeared. In today's world of shifting industry boundaries, the notion of telling a company to stick to its knitting seems akin to an order for corporate suicide. However, Peters doesn't mind changing his tune. He believes now that there are *no* excellent companies. He has modified the message. It is no longer enough to be excellent: companies have to stand out from the crowd. Companies have to shrink, even deconstruct. They have to innovate. They must make the workplace more interesting.

Old structures are redundant. They are obstructing progress. In *Liberation Management* (1992) Peters pronounced the death of middle management with the sentence: "…[M]iddle managers as we have known them are cooked geese." The individual employee increasingly has to brand himself or herself. He prophesies an increasing number of women workers and welcomes this: Women are better than men at working in teams.

He believes that "90 percent of white-collar jobs will be totally reinvented/reconceived in the next decade." His interest in crafting the new corporate citizen led to the production of a series of books including *The Brand You 50* (1999) and *Project 50* (1999).

Peters is a consummate performer, injecting the same messianism into his public appearances as is found in his books. A lecture by Tom Peters is a performance, a spectacle even. He is never static. Someone (at an obvious loose end) once calculated that he walks seven miles on stage while giving a lecture. He gives about 100 talks a year throughout the world. He jokes that that's why he called his first horse "Frequent Flyer."

Tom Peters and Robert Waterman were also instrumental in the development of the 7-S method of isolating management strengths and weaknesses, developed with Richard Pascale and Tony Athos.

Essential reading

http://tompeters.com
In Search of Excellence (Harper & Row, 1982) (with Robert H. Waterman)
A Passion for Excellence: The Leadership Difference (Warner, 1985) (with Nancy Austin)
Thriving on Chaos: Handbook for a Management Revolution (Knopf, 1987)
Liberation Management: Necessary Disorganization for the Nanosecond Nineties (Knopf, 1992)
The Brand You 50 (Knopf, 1999)
Re-Imagine (Dorling Kindersley, 2003)

MICHAEL PORTER
Educator (2005 Ranking: 1)

Michael E. Porter (born 1947) is the Bishop William Laurence University Professor at the Harvard Business School. He has an almost "living legend" status in the world of management thinking. He has written 18 books and countless articles. In addition to his teaching, he consults widely with the Monitor Group which he helped establish. Above all he is an educator, either by the spoken or by the written word; however, he is not a performer or management superstar. *The Economist* once commented that he was not likely to write a best-selling management blockbuster. His books are "heavy," which probably explains why few of them are available in paperback. He has advised both the public and private sectors throughout the world. Not only has he been showered with academic and business awards, he has even received civic medals usually reserved for military heroes or extraordinary sports people. Porter was for many years active in the U.S. military's reserve and was a celebrated college footballer, baseballer, and golfer in his youth.

Porter was born in a university town, Ann Arbor, Michigan. His father was an army officer. Porter studied mechanical and aerospace engineering at Princeton and then switched to business, earning an M.B.A. and a Ph.D. in economics from Harvard. He later joined the faculty there.

Porter has always been obsessed by competition. His first widely read book *Competitive Strategy* (1980) is now in its 63rd imprint. In it he analyzes competition. There is:

+ Natural competition and tension between existing players in an industry
+ The threat of new entrants to the market

- The prospect of substitute products or services
- The bargaining power of suppliers
- The bargaining power of consumers

There are three ways to compete effectively:

- Produce a product or service more cheaply
- Produce something that is better and different from the competition, defining this as "differentiation"
- Dominate a niche market and close out the competitors

Porter did not believe many companies could do all three or even two at a time. The particular strategy chosen depended on what type of company you had. He noted five types:

- Global
- Fragmented
- Emerging
- Mature
- Declining

The company also had to look at the series of links that went into its provision or production. He called this the value chain (and the name has stuck). He isolated five primary activities in any value chain:

- Internal logistics: getting the necessary materials
- Production or provision
- External logistics and distribution
- Marketing
- After-sales services

These were each accompanied by a range of secondary activities: each company's value chain in turn fitted into a wider value system.

Porter subsequently moved from competition between firms to competition between nations. In *The Competitive Advantage of Nations* (1990) he examined why some states were wealthy and others were not. The important element here was national value systems. He visualized these as akin to a four-sided diamond. The four components were:

+ Domestic rivalry: the tougher, the better
+ Traditional economic resources
+ Infrastructure, including the education level of its citizens
+ The cluster phenomenon

The last point is very important, though frequently overlooked. These are concentrations of particular types of industry in defined geographical areas, such as low-tech Portuguese cork-makers and Silicon Valley. These areas can use economies of scale to attract workers and increase efficiency, as well as cross-subsidization and skills pools.

His study of national economies has been extensive, though not always welcome. In *Can Japan Compete?* (2000) he showed that the long and protracted recession suffered by Japan was the inevitable result of successive post-war Japanese governments' policies.

His most recent research on competition has involved a look at America's inner cities. He argues that wealth creation is a more sound panacea for poverty and inequality reduction than redistributing wealth from elsewhere.

Porter has academically colonized much of the east coast of the United States with various centers supplied with full-time research staff working on a plethora of projects dear to his academic heart, from competition to inner-city development.

Essential reading

http://dor.hbs.edu/fi_redirect.jhtml?facInfo=bio&facEmId=mporter&loc=extn

Competitive Strategy Techniques for Analyzing Industries and Competitors (Free Press, 1980)

Comparative Advantage (Free Press, 1985)

The Competitive Advantage of Nations (Free Press, 1990)

Can Japan Compete? (Palgrave Macmillan, 2000)

C. K. PRAHALAD
Educator (2005 Ranking: 3)
....

Coimbatore Krishnao Prahalad was born in 1941 in the town of Coimbatore in Tamil Nadu, India. He studied physics at the University of Madras (now Chenai), followed by work as a manager in a branch of the Union Carbide battery company, where he gained experience in management. He continued his education in the U.S., earning a Ph.D. from Harvard. He taught both in India and in America, eventually joining the faculty of the University of Michigan's Business School, where he holds the Harvey C. Fruehauf Chair of Business Administration.

At Ann Arbor he met Gary Hamel, then a young international business student. Their collaboration ultimately resulted in *Competing for the Future* (1995). This book described how the status quo in management was in transition. It was moving from the old control-and-command model toward one where managers had to find new market opportunities. Much depended on markets and the delivery of customer satisfaction. This was in contrast to the concept of business process reengineering, which told companies to look for core competencies.

In his most recent book, *The Future of Competition* (2004), written with Venkat Ramaswamy, Prahalad argues that companies have not made enough use of the opportunities provided by globalization. There is an inability to realize that not only have the rules of the game changed but the role of the players has been transformed too. The customer is a more powerful and proactive figure, no longer an abstraction that has to be satisfied. Thanks to the Internet, customers are agents creating and participating in transactions. The concept of value has also changed. It is not inherent in products or services. It cannot be instilled by producers or providers. It has to be co-created with consumers. They build value by experiencing it. The only way companies can compete successfully is through building new strategic capital.

Prahalad desired a more hands-on approach to business. In 1997 he co-founded Praja (Sanskrit for "common people") in San Diego. This Internet start-up wanted to pull the Internet away from information-based content

towards something more experiential. The company's fortunes were badly hit by the puncturing of the tech bubble. Prahalad commented philosophically that this experience had taught him a lot.

Prahalad maintains a deep interest in the world's poor. This led him to write *The Fortune at the Bottom of the Pyramid* (2004). It stemmed from a "long and lonely journey" to find a solution to the world's poverty. He identified the world's poor (the bottom of the pyramid, or BOP) as a potential untapped market for companies, worth anything up to $13 trillion a year: "The real source of market promise is not the wealthy few in the developing world, or even the emerging middle-income consumers. It is the billions of aspiring poor who are joining the market economy for the first time."

A market at the bottom of the pyramid could be co-created by multinational and domestic industry, non-governmental organizations, and – most importantly – *the poor themselves.* They would then have choice over their lives and the products they used. Prahalad pointed to Hindustan Lever's success in marketing soap-powder and detergents in smaller, cheaper units. This created prosperity downstream through new distribution mechanisms. The book is accompanied by a CD-ROM containing interviews with people whose lives have been improved. Prahalad's interest has nothing to do with philanthropy. He says that too often poor people are patronized by aid agencies. He wants them to have real power in the marketplace.

His book also highlights the victimization of the poor in some areas. In India there persists a "poverty penalty," where poor Indian families are forced into the arms of money-lenders charging interest rates in excess of 400 percent.

Essential reading

http://www.thenextpractice.com/who_we_are/ck_prahalad_founding_
  partner_ceo.php

Competing for the Future (Harvard Business School Press, 1995) (with Gary
  Hamel)

The Future of Competition: Co-Creating Unique Value With Customers (Harvard Business School Press, 2004) (with Venkat Ramaswamy)

The Fortune at the Bottom of the Pyramid: Eradicating Poverty Through Profits
  (Wharton, 2004)

EDGAR H. SCHEIN
Educator (2005 Ranking: 36)

Edgar Schein (born 1928) is Sloan Fellows Professor of Management Emeritus and former Professor of Organization Psychology and Management at the Massachusetts Institute of Technology (M.I.T.). Although he has now retired, he still teaches there part-time.

He studied psychology at the University of Chicago and received a doctorate in social psychology from Harvard.

He saw active service as a captain in the U.S. Army in Korea, experience that proved seminal for much of his later work. Afterward he joined the faculty of the Sloan School of Management at M.I.T. and has never left.

Schein became interested in brainwashing. He observed its effects on American prisoners of war in Korea. He also saw parallels with the training provided by companies like GE and IBM in their in-house training facilities. Employees were taught to identify totally with the company and its aims. What was happening in GE or IBM was the indoctrination of a culture.

He has also been interested in the behavior of groups. He is considered to be the first to coin the term "corporate culture." He defined this in *Organizational Culture and Leadership* (1985) as "... a pattern of basic assumptions – invented, discovered or developed by a group as it learns to cope with its problems of external adaptation and internal integration [and that is] considered valid and [is] taught to new members as the correct way ..."

These basic assumptions are based on:

+ Humanity's relationship to nature: do we control it, or does it control us?
+ What is truth: does it emerge through debate and experiment, or are truth and reality imposed from above?

+ What is human nature: is it manipulative, trying to get the biggest output from the smallest input? Or is it striving for bigger ideals?
+ Why do we do what we do: in the Western world, achievement and finishing the task are important, but other cultures have different attitudes toward work.
+ How do we deal with other humans: is interaction a good thing? Does our organization encourage or discourage it?

These dimensions, like culture, are dynamic – in a constant state of development and adaptation.

A culture can be created by a corporate founding father and may be maintained by his descendants. A forceful CEO can have a similar impact. This type of culture is usually tied closely to these individuals' values.

Culture changes as the organization changes. There are roughly three stages in the organization's development: (1) birth and early growth, (2) organizational midlife, and (3) organizational maturity.

Management has a subset of cultures. There are three that Schein identifies as central to organizational learning, which must always be kept in balance:

+ The operator culture: "an internal culture based on operational success"
+ The engineering culture: maintained by those "who drive the organization's core competencies"
+ The executive culture: maintained by the organization's top echelons

Schein is also known for his writings about careers in organizations, especially for coining the term *psychological contract*. This contract is based on the unspoken assumption that managerial employees would work hard and conscientiously. They would be loyal to the organization and obedient to those in higher positions. In return they would receive lifetime employment. This psychological contract produced the company man; there were few women. Originality and creativity were unwelcome extras. The organization had a quasi-military structure. It was accepted because, in its heyday of the 1950s and 1960s, people remembered the hardships and uncertainties of the Depression years. They had also experienced real military discipline in World War II or (like Schein) in Korea. In return, managers gained a predictable and respectable lifestyle. The psychological contract was a white-collar phenomenon, and it did not apply to the blue-collar ranks.

The psychological contract increasingly belongs to history. Companies want bright and creative people who, they hope, will also be fairly loyal and hard working. Potential managers no longer see as desirable the predictability of lifelong employment in the same firm. They want to take nectar from a whole range of different flowers. Getting managers to stay is now the issue: coercive persuasion is no longer an option.

Essential reading

http://web.mit.edu/scheine/www/bio.html
Career Dynamics: Watching Individual and Organizational Needs (Addison Wesley, 1978)
Organizational Culture (Jossey-Bass, 1980)
Organizational Culture and Leadership (Jossey-Bass, 1985)
The Corporate Culture Survival Guide (Jossey-Bass, 1999)

RICARDO SEMLER
Executive (2005 Ranking: 37)

Ricardo Semler (born 1959) is the largest shareholder and "non CEO" of the Brazilian manufacturer Semco. Ricardo's father, an Austrian engineer, founded the company, based in Sao Paulo, in 1954. It originally made marine pumps but has expanded in all directions including real estate, retail, and information technology.

His father gave Ricardo control of the company in 1980. At first he ran the firm in a fairly traditional way. However, poor health brought on by high stress, combined with a lack of motivation by staff, persuaded him to introduce some radical changes.

Conventional wisdom might have suggested pursuing efficiencies through cost cutting, maybe closing down altogether, but Semler threw away the management rulebook.

He is fond of quoting a parable about three medieval stonecutters who were asked to provide job descriptions: The first said that he cut stones; the second that he carved stones into intricate designs; the third answered that he built cathedrals. Semler has tried to promote the "cathedral builders" on his staff by giving them real responsibility and instituting on-the-job democracy.

Management should trust its workforce, so security checks on employees were dispensed with early on. A system of factory committees was established that decide everything from catering issues to product lines. Semler found at the beginning that trust was a two-way process. Employees, long used to taking orders and keeping their mouths closed, were afraid that the changes were ephemeral, and that they might be punished for speaking their minds. Semler assured them that no one would be fired, and so the reforms took hold.

Management has taken a back seat. The culture of oppression was first abolished. Management lost titles, offices, secretaries, even designated desks from which they could work. Semco workers can set production targets themselves. They are encouraged to continually ask "Why?" Work is no longer dominated by a single transaction – sale of labor in return for wages. Instead, it is a creative environment in which workers set their own goals and are responsible for their attainment. Anyone who wishes can belong to a union, and strikes sometimes occur. A new relationship has been fostered between workers and management. Supervisors are chosen by the people whom they manage.

Semler sees his approach as having little to do with management theory. It is an application of sociology and anthropology to the workplace. Many saw it as a recipe for chaos and predicted its imminent demise. Semco's results have proven otherwise. Profits went from a respectable $32 million when Ricardo took over to $160 million in 2002. Employment went from 90 to over 3,000 in the same period.

Semler does not believe in growth as a goal. Companies should grow to offset things like inflation. It should be like Semco's growth: organic, not forced.

Commentators who used to say "it will end in tears" increasingly say "it could never happen anywhere else." Semco has entered into partnerships with companies throughout the world and has taken over others.

Semco remains a private company. That way Semler and his fellow thinkers keep control of its agenda. Were it to go public, it would mean transferring power to analysts and institutional investors who would not have the interests of his staff at heart.

His workers have established several successful spin-offs on their own initiative. Semler insists that he is no longer in charge – he is "gainfully unemployed" since the company seems to run itself.

Semler's views on work are unorthodox. He says there is too big a contrast between work and leisure and that the opposite of work is not leisure, but idleness. Free time is often a time of creativity, listening, and responding to instincts.

Semler has given lectures and talks all over the world, often to leading businessmen. He does not think much of traditional business education, saying it is overly cerebral, with no place for emotions. He has applied his educational thinking outside the company, setting up a school with the same participative spirit as that of Semco.

Essential reading

http://edition.cnn.com/2004/BUSINESS/06/29/semler.profile/

Maverick: The Success Story Behind the World's Most Unusual Workplace (Warner, 1994)

The Seven-Day Weekend: Feeding Ducks and Making Millions (Portfolio, 2003)

PETER SENGE
Educator (2005 Ranking: 23)

....

Peter Senge (born 1947) is the director of the Center for Organizational Learning at the Massachusetts Institute of Technology (M.I.T.) and chairperson of the Society for Organizational Learning (SoL). He studied engineering at Stanford. After graduation he went to M.I.T. to complete his doctoral studies. In addition to his teaching and writing, Senge consults. He was a founding partner of Innovation Associates, now part of Arthur D. Little.

Senge popularized the notion of the learning organization in his book *The Fifth Discipline* (1990), though the term was first used by Chris Argyris over a decade earlier. Senge sums up the learning organization as "a group of people who are continually enhancing their capability to create their future." It is the best way for a company to come to terms with a rapidly changing world. It involves an approach to learning going far deeper than the simple once-and-for-all digestion of information. Learning is "about changing individuals so that they produce results they care about, accomplish things that are important to them."

The learning organization for Senge is characterized by a number of elements:

+ Personal mastery and self-discipline
+ Continual challenging of stereotypes on all levels
+ Shared vision
+ Team learning
+ Shared purpose

* Alignment
* Systemic thinking

Every organization has, among its members, vast potential for learning. This has to be harnessed at every level. Managers have to change from being overseers to being agents and inciters of change. They must learn how their companies work and suggest how they might work better. Everyone must communicate without fear. Learning comes through dialogue and discussion, but the two are not the same: discussion is always more focused. This produces information that causes action, resulting in a new pool of information. Therefore, learning has an effect not unlike throwing a pebble in a pond. Learning is about understanding the linkages between sometimes quite disparate things.

"As the world becomes more interconnected and business becomes more complex and dynamic, work must become more *learningful*," according to Senge. People have to be encouraged to experiment. Learning occurs through mistakes.

In spite of the book's popularity, Senge was disappointed with companies' responses. They either paid no more than lip service to it or turned their backs on his learning strategies altogether. Many corporations were mistake-averse, often punishing those making mistakes even when the errors were relatively harmless.

He realized that one of the most change-averse elements within an organization is its culture. It can often survive downsizing or reengineering with remarkable tenacity but new forms of learning cannot go far in the face of cultural hostility. In *The Dance of Change* (1999) Senge reflected on these failures, arguing that understanding of the factors that are obstructing change is needed first. Senge isolated three elements that promote change. He also found ten reasons for doing nothing or for moving backwards. He hints that the forces of inertia within an organization may be so great that they frustrate even the most driven CEO. But some of the obstacles can be redrawn to help develop a learning organization. For example, an excuse for not adopting a change initiative is often "lack of time." If this is taken sincerely, it can be an opportunity to reframe the use of time within the organization as a whole. As in *The Fifth Discipline*, Senge offers practical advice and strategies for overcoming these obstacles.

His latest book, *Presence* (2005), is based on hundreds of interviews with businessmen, academics, and scientists on the nature of change and their ways of dealing with it. It presents a radically new approach to learning. Senge and his co-authors point to new ways of seeing and sensing.

Senge is dismissive of much of management thinking and writing. Anyone seeking insight into business management is like one of the explorers during the great ages of discovery, he says. They have an idea of where they want to go, but they have inadequate maps for the journey, with only a collection of very uneven and contradictory notes from earlier voyagers – the equivalents of most recent writing on management. He believes that these should not be dismissed out of hand, however; they are better than nothing and may contain kernels of reliability.

Essential reading

http://www.solonline.org/aboutsol/who/Senge/

The Fifth Discipline: The Art and Practice of the Learning Organization (Currency, 1990)

The Dance of Change: The Challenges of Sustaining Momentum in Learning Organizations (Currency, 1999)

Presence: Exploring Profound Change in People, Organizations and Society (Currency, 2005) (with C. Otto Scharmer, Joseph Jaworuki and Betty Sue Flowers)

THOMAS A. STEWART

Journalist (2005 Ranking: 13)

....

Thomas A. Stewart is the founder of the concepts of knowledge management and intellectual capital exploitation.

He graduated with a major in English literature from Harvard in 1970 and then pursued a career in the publishing world. He was president of Atheneum Publishing before leaving to become a journalist. He joined the editorial board of *Fortune*, contributing many pieces on a variety of topics. He is best known as the author of "The Leading Edge" column, read by almost a million people.

Stewart is versatile; he has shown himself ready to write on almost any topic. The topic for which he is most famous is knowledge.

There was a time, not so long ago, when terms like intellectual capital and the knowledge economy were practically unknown. Anyone who had read Peter Drucker's *Age of Discontinuity* (1969) closely was aware of the concept of the knowledge worker, but for many people these were unfamiliar terms. However, the advent of the Information Age changed many doubters into believers. The book that described what was going on was Stewart's *Intellectual Capital* (1997). He argued that a fundamental shift in productive forces was taking place as great as that of the Industrial Revolution. Firms would no longer be able to rely on traditional bricks-and-mortar notions of capital, like equipment and land; the new and very powerful forms of capital were knowledge and skills or *intellectual capital*. It had "become the one indispensable asset of corporations."

Intellectual capital was more than the collective brainpower of an organization; it was brainpower harnessed and applied toward specific ends: "Organizational intellect becomes intellectual capital only when it can be deployed to do something that could not be done if it remained scattered around like so many coins in a gutter." It is "useful knowledge packed for others."

In Stewart's thinking there are three varieties:

+ Human capital: implicit knowledge
+ Customer capital: the value of relationships between customer and company
+ Structural capital: "... knowledge that doesn't go home at night" including processes and systems – the information that an organization acquires over a business lifetime

The rise of intellectual capital has important implications for all in an organization. It gives those with the new knowledge a whole host of career choices:

+ Careers can no longer be seen as a series of steps up the corporate pyramid
+ Project management is the furnace in which successful careers are forged
+ Power will flow from expertise, not position
+ Most roles in the knowledge-based organization can be performed equally well by outsiders as by insiders
+ Careers are made in markets
+ Career choices are not made between companies, but between specialization and generalization
+ Intellectual capital is a source of wealth both for companies and for individuals; it is held in common between the two

Stewart also prophesied the end, or at least the radical transformation, of management. The knowledge workers are the people who know best how to apply their skills and know-how, not managers. Their work has to be assessed by goals attained, not by tasks performed.

Stewart says that it is up to companies to mine the intellectual skills available within their organizations through effective knowledge management systems. Many tried, but were often at a loss to know how to do it; others paid lip service to the concepts involved. Knowledge management seemed destined to join the ranks of the Management Idea of the Month. Many felt that the fault lay partially with Stewart, whose book had been a little short on hard details. So, in his next book, *The Wealth of Knowledge* (2003), he outlined four simple steps companies should take to make the most of their intellectual capital:

+ Identify and evaluate the role of knowledge in the business
+ Match the revenues with the knowledge assets that produce them
+ Develop a strategy for investing in and exploiting the firm's intellectual assets
+ Improve the efficiency of knowledge work and knowledge workers

Essential reading

http://members.aol.com/thosstew/bio.html
Intellectual Capital: The New Wealth of Organizations (Currency, 1997)
The Wealth of Knowledge: Intellectual Capital and the Twenty-first Century Organization (Currency, 2003)

FONS TROMPENAARS AND CHARLES HAMPDEN-TURNER

Consultants (2005 Ranking: 25)

Fons Trompenaars and Charles Hampden-Turner are managing directors of Trompenaars Hampden-Turner Intercultural Management Consultancy (formerly the Centre for International Business Studies), based in Amsterdam. They have collaborated for over two decades on detailed research into cultural differences between markets.

Fons Trompenaars studied economics at the Vrije Universiteit in Amsterdam. He went on to the University of Pennsylvania's Wharton School of Finance for his doctorate. He then worked for nine years with Royal Dutch Shell. In addition to his consultancy work, he is a visiting professor at the Erasmus University in Rotterdam.

Charles Hampden-Turner studied at the University of Cambridge, gaining his doctorate in the Harvard Business School. He too worked for Royal Dutch Shell, where he was involved in group planning. He taught for many years, both in the U.S. and at the London Business School, and is now Senior Research Associate in International and Strategic Management in the Judge Institute of Management Studies in Cambridge.

Trompenaars and Hampden-Turner began their research into cultural nuances among managers in a rigorous and analytical way, sending out 15,000 questionnaires to managers in 28 countries. They extrapolated their findings into their theory of value dimensions. These are six cultural parameters, or mirror images. Each one contains two bipolar attitudinal opposites about the world. These are:

+ Universalist – particularist
+ Individualist – communitarian
+ Specificity – diffuseness
+ Achieved status – ascribed status
+ Inner direction – external direction
+ Time is sequential – time is synchronous

They found that some countries veered more towards one side of the value dimension than the other. Individualism and universalism were prevalent in the United States and Canada, while a communitarian, collectivist viewpoint dominated in Japan and in Southeast Asia. The value dimensions should not be viewed as geographic generalizations, however. Both sides could be evident in one country, even in the same company.

All parts of the value dimension matrix have their plus and minus points. Individualism breeds good leaders at all levels. It can also foster greed and selfishness. Communitarianism promotes a sense of belonging, a willingness to make sacrifices, and a belief in something beyond the individual. This may be called society, and it is greater than its constituent parts. It may retard innovation and be slow to change in the face of altered external conditions.

Value dimensions should be looked at in an unbiased way. Those wanting to deal with them must be able to look both ways, to see and understand in a circular fashion. This is the secret to cross-cultural management. It is possible to try to reconcile the different extremes of the value dimension. This can make the best of both worlds.

In their numerous books Trompenaars and Hampden-Turner give examples of good circular thinking in action. One of these is from the American sales division of IBM. Sales personnel were rewarded on quantity of sales. There was considerable competition among staff to get the best sales figures. This led to unwanted pressure on buyers who felt they were being hassled by sales staff. It also led to friction and a lot of stress. This was a classic case of predominant or out-of-balance individualism. IBM called in consultants in response to rising stress levels, absenteeism, and complaints. The consultants suggested scrapping the compensation system based on individual sales figures. Instead rewards should go to the salesperson who had learned most from the buyers. This could be tested by the salespeople giving presentations to their colleagues, who would then vote for which presentation suggested that the most had been learned. This was a more communitarian approach. When it was implemented, the sales people were happy, stress levels and absenteeism dropped, and so did complaints from buyers about overeager salespeople. It was also found that the winners in this new environment were the best salespeople according to the old individualist system.

Conflicts between values are universal and ubiquitous, but different value dimensions can be reconciled. Those societies and organizations in which this has occurred are usually healthier, wealthier, and wiser. They point to a new road to wealth, not through value added, but through value reconciled.

Essential reading

http://www.7d-culture.nl/index1.html
Riding the Waves of Culture: Understanding Cultural Diversity in Business (McGraw-Hill, 1997)
Building Cross-cultural Competence: How to Create Wealth from Conflicting Values (Yale University Press, 2000)
Managing People Across Cultures (Culture for Business) (Capstone, 2004)

JACK WELCH
Executive (2005 Ranking: 5)

Jack Welch (born 1935) is the former CEO of General Electric. Born in Salem, Massachusetts, the son of a bus conductor, he studied chemical engineering at the University of Massachusetts, gaining a Ph.D. in the same subject from the University of Illinois. He joined General Electric's plastics division in 1960 and devoted the rest of his working life to the company.

His rise was meteoric. At age 33 he became one of the company's youngest general managers. He subsequently served as vice president and sector executive for the consumer products and services sector and finally was vice chairman and executive officer. In December 1980, after a little over 20 years in the company, he was named GE's eighth CEO, the youngest in the company's history.

Welch had an immense impact on corporate America, setting standards of best practice for its senior executives. He always led by example. He had pioneered the potential of GE's plastics divisions. He also laid the foundation for the success of GE Capital. As CEO he took a number of innovative steps to promote the disparate elements of what had become an unwieldy conglomerate. Welch announced to the various sectors that, unless they could become either number one or two in their respective industries, they would be spun off. He commented, "My main job was developing talent. I was a gardener providing water and other nourishment to our top 750 people. Of course, I had to pull out some weeds, too." He also introduced the practice of establishing "anti-groups" within certain divisions whose role was to put forward the opposite to official policy in a deliberate attempt to encourage debate and discourage group thinking.

He earned a reputation for being endlessly creative, never being hide-bound by convention when it came to solving a problem.

He introduced Six Sigma Quality Management at GE, after its usefulness had been shown in Motorola. He was an early advocate of Six Sigma, a means of achieving near-perfection in manufacturing by gradual, incremental steps, monitored by specially trained experts called Black Belts and Master Black Belts.

Welch also became known for his desire to communicate. He is reputed to have written three to four thousand notes to members of his staff every year. GE's financial success came at the expense of extensive layoffs. During the process of streamlining the company, over 100,000 workers lost their jobs. His perceived ruthlessness earned him the moniker "Neutron Jack." He hated bureaucracy in any form and always sought people who were dedicated to change. He was also an active teacher at the GE Leadership Center in Crotonville, New York.

After nearly two decades at the helm, Welch prepared for his departure and a smooth succession. The person who was to take up his mantle was chosen from within the GE organization, through a long and rigorous proc-ess. This resulted in the anointing of Jeffrey Immelt as the prospective CEO in April 2001 when Welch promised to "walk away and keep walking." Things did not go according to plan, however. GE had acquired Honeywell in 1990, and Welch announced he wanted to stay in charge to oversee its integration. However, the takeover was scuttled when the European Commission raised objections that the resultant company would have a dominant and potentially distorting role in the aviation-financing sector in Europe. Welch was thus denied a last charge towards the setting sun. Most observers felt this did not do him any harm. At GE he was a larger-than-life figure.

Since retiring, Welch has continued to consult to a number of Fortune 500 firms. He also found the time to write his memoirs, *Jack: Straight from the Gut* (2001), which became the number one best-selling book in the U.S. (Outside the U.S. the book had the less macho subtitle of *What I've Learned Leading a Great Company and Great People.*) He has since added *Winning: The Ultimate Business How-To Book* (2005). This "…is a book for the people in business who sweat, get their nails dirty, hire, fire, make hard decisions, and pay the price when those decisions are wrong."

Essential reading

http://www.jackwelchwinning.com/biojack.html
Jack: Straight from the Gut (Warner, 2001) (with John A. Byrne)
Winning: The Ultimate Business How-To Book (Collins, 2005) (with Suzy Welch)

ASSEMBLING
THE 50

....

Thinkers 50 2005 (2003 ranking in brackets)

....

 1 Michael PORTER (2)
 2 Bill GATES (20)
 3 C.K. PRAHALAD (12)
 4 Tom PETERS (3)
 5 Jack WELCH (8)
 6 Jim COLLINS (10)
 7 Philip KOTLER (6)
 8 Henry MINTZBERG (7)
 9 Kjell NORDSTRÖM and Jonas RIDDERSTRÅLE (21)
10 Charles HANDY (5)
11 Richard BRANSON (34)
12 Scott ADAMS (27)
13 Thomas STEWART (37)
14 Gary HAMEL (4)
15 Chan KIM and Renée MAUBORGNE (31)
16 Kenichi OHMAE (19)
17 Patrick DIXON (46)
18 Stephen COVEY (16)
19 Rosabeth MOSS KANTER (9)
20 Edward DE BONO (35)

21 Clayton CHRISTENSEN (22)
22 Robert KAPLAN and David NORTON (15)
23 Peter SENGE (14)
24 Ram CHARAN (–)
25 Fons TROMPENAARS adn Charles HAMPDEN-TURNER(50)
26 Russell ACKOFF (–)
27 Warren BENNIS (13)
28 Chris ARGYRIS (18)
29 Michael DELL (33)
30 Vijay GOVINDARAJAN (–)
31 Malcolm GLADWELL (–)
32 Manfred KETS DE VRIES (43)
33 Rakesh KHURANA (–)
34 Lynda GRATTON (41)
35 Alan GREENSPAN (42)
36 Edgar SCHEIN (17)
37 Ricardo SEMLER (36)
38 Don PEPPERS (48)
39 Paul KRUGMAN (40)
40 Jeff BEZOS (39)
41 Andy GROVE (26)
42 Daniel GOLEMAN (29)
43 Leif EDVINSSON (–)
44 James CHAMPY and Michael HAMMER (25)
45 Rob GOFFEE and Gareth JONES (–)
46 Naomi KLEIN (30)
47 Geert HOFSTEDE (47)
48 Larry BOSSIDY (–)
49 Costas MARKIDES (–)
50 Geoffrey MOORE (38)

Who is the most influential living management thinker?

Visitors to the Thinkers 50 website (www.thinkers50.com) have been providing their answers. The Thinkers 50 team also e-mailed hundreds of business people, consultants, academics, and M.B.A. students throughout the world. After sifting through more than 1,200 votes, a list of contenders was compiled.

The result was a short list of 80 names. A Google search was then undertaken to establish the number of references for each of those on the list, and factored into the ranking. Finally, they were assessed against ten criteria on a scale of 1 (low) to 10 (high).

The measures

1 Originality of ideas
Are the ideas and examples used by the thinker original?

2 Practicality of ideas
Have the ideas promoted by the thinker been implemented in organizations? And, has the implementation been successful?

3 Presentation style
How proficient is the thinker at presenting his/her ideas orally?

4 Written communication
How proficient is the thinker at presenting his/her ideas in writing?

5 Loyalty of followers
How committed are the thinker's disciples to spreading the message and putting it to work?

6 Business sense
Do they practice what they preach in their own business?

7 International outlook
How international are they in outlook and thinking?

8 Rigor of research
How well researched are their books and presentations?

9 *Impact of ideas*
Have their ideas had an impact on the way people manage or think about management?

10 *Guru factor*
The clincher: are they, for better or worse, guru material by your definition and expectation?

INDEX

· ·